G
PLANTI

D1066179

Popular Exotic Cacti in colour

By Edgar Lamb
THE ILLUSTRATED REFERENCE ON CACTI AND
OTHER SUCCULENTS
Volume 1 (1955, 1958, 1963, 1969, 1973)
Volume 2 (1959, 1968, 1973, 1974)
Volume 3 (1963) (with Brian Lamb)
Volume 4 (1966, 1971, 1974) (with Brian Lamb)
STAPELIADS IN CULTIVATION (1957) O/P
THE FLOWERING OF YOUR CACTI (1955) O/P
CACTI FROM SEED – THE EASY WAY (1959) O/P

By Edgar and Brian Lamb
POCKET ENCYCLOPAEDIA OF CACTI IN COLOUR
INCLUDING OTHER SUCCULENTS (1969, 1970, 1971, 1972)
COLOURFUL CACTI AND OTHER
SUCCULENTS OF THE DESERTS (1974, 1975)

Popular Exotic Cacti

in colour

Edgar and Brian Lamb

Edgar Lamb

Brian Lamb

Blandford Press
Poole Dorset

First published in 1975

© Blandford Press Ltd
Link House, West Street, Poole, Dorset BH15 1LL

ISBN 0 7137 0742 9

Printed and bound in Great Britain by Jarrold & Sons Ltd, Norwich

Contents

Introduction

The importance of a hobby is increasing as people have more and more leisure time, and hobbies connected with natural history are booming. The increase in the number of cacti enthusiasts around the world is reflected by the number of societies which are now in existence in almost every country from England, where this hobby started, to countries such as Russia and Japan. Fortunately this growing interest has made people more aware of their native flora and the need for conservation.

Another factor is that most cacti and other succulents originate in the type of environment where the degree of atmospheric humidity is very low, so these plants are far more suited to centrally heated homes than many of the house plants which have been grown in recent years. Although the majority of cacti do not actually need a high minimum temperature in winter, they will not die as a result of it, although it can adversely affect their flowering qualities in the following season. Ideally these plants will do best in a small greenhouse, a conservatory or a sunroom; it is also possible to grow them very well in a cellar using artificial lighting, whilst a variety of carefully chosen species can be grown in a raised rockery in the garden for twelve months of the year, even though they will be subjected to snow and ice during the winter.

Many people may not realise that although cacti are only native to the Americas or the New World a vast range of other succulent plants are to be found in almost every country in the world including, believe it or not, such chilly parts of the world as Greenland, the alpine areas of Switzerland and the Caucasus, and even in the Himalayas. It is true to say that by far the majority of these succulent plants are to be found in Africa and the surrounding islands as well as in the Americas, but there are also many species in India, Sri Lanka (Ceylon), Burma, China, many of the islands in the Pacific Ocean and Australia.

This book illustrates one plant from each of one hundred different genera, with a page or half page of text describing not only where the species in a certain genus occur in habitat, but also the basic features of that genus. It should be possible to place a plant in its correct genus (shown by the first name) with the aid of the non-technical text which accompanies each of the illustrations.

The main problem has been the selection of the genera to be included, and we are quite certain that someone will say, 'Why did you not include such and such a genus?' We have included more true cacti than other succulents, but we have endeavoured to include flowering plants, wherever this is really important for easy identification. We have also shown a selection of genera of which certain members are suitable for use as house plants. A few genera such as Sedums and Sempervivums, many of which can be grown outside rather like alpine plants, are included as well as some species of hardy cacti.

The text and illustrations are arranged as far as possible in alphabetical sequence by the generic name, and to aid pronunciation of these scientific names a phonetic key is provided. Following the scientific name is the abbreviated name of the person who first described it under that generic heading, the magnification and the family in which the genus belongs. We have included common names where possible, but in many cases there are no reliable ones which can be used with any degree of accuracy, as the names refer to more than one kind of plant. Where a scientific term is used an explanation of the term will be found alongside it in brackets, but the use of these terms has been minimised as far as possible.

Where to grow them In temperate climates such as that of Britain a greenhouse or conservatory is the best place, because you can control the watering requirements quite simply, and during the better months of the year the temperature can easily rise to over 100 °F (38 °C) or more during the daytime, which is ideal for the majority of cacti and other succulent plants. In fact when grown in this way, many species require some shade in cultivation, to imitate to a certain degree the conditions they seek in nature. In the text accompanying the illustrations you will often see a reference to the fact that certain plants grow beneath other bushes and trees. To shade a greenhouse or conservatory, no matter whether it is made of glass or plastic, is an easy matter. The expensive way is to use roller-blinds but the cheaper way to do it, most suited for a greenhouse in particular, is to white-wash the exterior of the glass lightly. This can be done either by splattering it on with a brush, or by means of a garden syringe. If some oil is added to the powdered whitening and water, it will stop it from being washed off so easily by heavy rain.

The position of your greenhouse is not too important, provided it receives sunshine for the major part of the day. West facing lean-to type greenhouses can be very successful, even though the sun may not alight on the plants until perhaps 11 am each day. The genus *Ferocactus* is one which enjoys sun and high temperatures, and yet we are growing and flowering very success-fully a number of species in a west facing lean-to greenhouse. So do not be deterred if you read in some books that greenhouses must be placed in a north–south aspect. We know of many enthusiasts who have a north facing conservatory, and although this limits to some extent their choice of species, they can still grow quite a variety of plants and flower them regularly.

Greenhouses and conservatories can be heated in winter by many methods today, so to a large extent it is a case of weighing up the costs and advantages of one method against another. Remember, by far the majority of the plants we are talking about can be grown in a greenhouse where the minimum temperature is only 45 °F (8 °C). Some require a little more and others can go down to 40 °F (5 °C) with complete safety. Obviously if you have a central heating system in your house an extra radiator or so is the cheapest method of heating, as the additional run-ning costs of the extra radiators will be very small, even though there is a greater heat loss from a room which is virtually 50 per cent glass. This can of course be reduced by lining it with plastic sheeting for the winter months, unless you have proper double-glazing. Electric tubular or fan heating systems, even with thermostats, are probably the most expensive methods of heating a conservatory or greenhouse, but nowadays it is possible to purchase small gas heaters (non-flued) which are run off natural gas, and this is definitely cheaper than electricity. The idea that gas fires are harmful to plant life is quite false, but is one of those old ideas which linger on. We have grown plants in our own homes under gas-fire conditions, for many years, as well as heating all our greenhouses in 'The Exotic Collection' at Worthing by gas convection heaters.

The cheapest method even today despite the rising cost of oil is the old paraffin heater and provided it is used properly, with regular cleaning of the wick and air-intake every week, it is ideal for the small greenhouse. It used to be necessary to refill it every day, but nowadays it is possible to purchase some kinds, specially made for the greenhouse, which by means of an extra tank do not need refilling more than every ten days or so.

Many cacti and other succulent plants are very suitable as house plants, either on sunny window-sills or, for some of the more shade-loving species, windows facing north. However, as the plants are only receiving light on one side, which is after all rather unnatural, it does pay to turn through 180° once or twice each week. Obviously under household conditions they will not be growing in the same hot environment that is likely in a greenhouse, so the amount of water required in summer will be less. In contrast, during the winter months they will probably be warmer than in the greenhouse, and will therefore require a little water occasionally to prevent shrivelling. Many of the true cacti do not flower so well if they have not rested during the winter months at a sufficiently low temperature, but this higher winter temperature can be beneficial for many of the other succulent plants.

If you do not have sufficient window-sill space it is possible today to purchase tubular Grolux lights under which all types of plant-life can be grown. We have seen a number of collections of cacti grown by this method in cellars. The owners can thus boast that their plants have never seen the light of day and yet we would have been proud to have grown those same plants as well under our own greenhouse conditions. It is possible to obtain books and pamphlets on this subject, although not actually referring to cacti, but the same principles apply.

Another fascinating side to this hobby is a raised alpine rockery for hardy cacti and other succulents. Such a rockery should be built in a position in the garden where the plants will receive plenty of sunshine, and if it can be against a south facing wall, all the better. For these plants to succeed outside, the soil must have very good drainage properties, so in addition to plenty of stones and shingle at the bottom, the soil mixture should consist of 2 or 3 parts of fine shingle, 1 or 2 of gritty sand, and only 1 of humus, topped off with a 1 in. (2·5 cm) layer of shingle around the plants. This layer ensures good drainage around the neck of each plant. This may seem a very poor soil mixture; however, it is quite sufficient for some of the hardy Opuntias such as *O. compressa, O. rhodantha, O. rafinesquei, O. polyacantha*, a few globular cacti like *Coryphantha vivipara* and *Neobesseya missouriensis*, and succulents such as certain Sedums, Sempervivums and the North American Lewisias. If the plants are too full of moisture when severe frosts start they are likely to suffer, but a shrivelled plant will survive.

Soil requirements Although it is possible to purchase plastic bags full of compost supposedly suitable for cacti, this is not always a good idea. Unfortunately today such ready-made mixtures are not necessarily reliable, so it usually pays to buy the ingredients and make it up yourself. It will also be much cheaper this way! Some books may lead you to believe that the soil requirements differ from genus to genus, but please do not believe this nonsense, as by far the majority of plants will grow in one simple mixture. We can say this from nearly fifty years' experience of the successful culture of these plants.

A very well rotted leafmould, made from beech or oak leaves or a mixture of the two, forms half of the ideal simple soil mixture. The second requirement is a gritty sand which is well washed, and will not set hard when it goes dry; one used by aquarium enthusiasts for their fish tanks is ideal. If you mix together equal parts (by volume) of the leafmould and sand and add nothing else, your plants will grow extremely well. If you have, or can obtain a good sifted loam, that is one which does not set hard when dry, one part of this can also be added to the above mixture if you wish, but it is not essential.

The alternative to the leafmould is to use peat. There are many kinds of peat but they are not always suitable for use with cacti for the following reason. Under normal greenhouse conditions, most cacti should be left dry for the winter period, and a soil made up with the wrong sort of peat can be very difficult to moisten again, when the plants are watered for the first time in the spring. We have found, however, that a sedge-peat has very similar moistening properties to a well rotted leafmould, so do bear this factor in mind when purchasing peat as an alternative to a good well rotted leafmould. If peat is used, additional nutrient is required as there is far less nourishment value in peat than in leafmould. It is possible to obtain the basic ingredients from a local firm which specialises in garden equipment, seeds and fertilisers.

We suggest the use of a teaspoon as a simple method of measuring, as the proportions in which the ingredients of this home-made fertiliser are mixed do not have to be exact.

To a one-gallon (4·5 litre) measure of the sand and peat mixture – add:

4 heaped teaspoons of *bone meal*
3 heaped teaspoons of *gypsum*
1 heaped teaspoon of *superphosphate*

This fertiliser can also be added to the leafmould and sand mixture, which will mean that a plant will not need repotting for four to five years, unless it becomes physically too big for the pot in which it is planted.

What to grow them in It is really essential to grow them in pots which have drainage holes; otherwise it is a very easy matter to over-water plants, which is the reason why great care has to be taken over watering bowl gardens. Today there are far more plastic than clay pots available, because plastic ones are cheaper to make and transport, being very light in weight. However, there are disadvantages to plastic pots. Some kinds become very brittle after a year or so in the greenhouse, so one must remember to put a hand around the pot when lifting it up after it is planted, instead of picking it up by the rim as one does with clay pots. The majority of the easier growing cacti and other succulents will grow equally well in plastic or clay, but there are some very slow growing species which we think are best grown in clay pots. A clay pot is porous, so that water is lost not only through the drainage holes at the bottom and by evaporation from the surface of the soil, but also through the porous clay surface of the pot itself. With a plastic pot this latter method of water loss is not possible. The fact is that with a climate like that of Britain where the summer weather cannot always be relied upon, plants may be watered on a warm day, but the following week may be dull and cool. In a plastic pot the soil will remain moist for a long time, whereas in a clay one it will lose the moisture at a faster rate, and this factor could make all the difference between losing a slow growing plant by rotting and keeping it alive.

How often to water cacti This is really the most difficult question of all to answer, and one which can only be learned by experience. Under normal greenhouse conditions with the plants grown in our suggested soil mixture in clay pots, most plants will require watering every 7–10 days in the spring and autumn, and every 4–5 days in the summer. If the plants are growing in plastic pots an extra two days can be added to the gaps between watering. Ideally in the growing season plants should be watered just as the soil mixture is about to become completely dry, but if in doubt leave them for an extra day or so. If the pots are standing on a wooden staging or a similar flat smooth surface, they are ready for watering when no water has been visible on this flat surface for a day.

The best and really the only method of watering any of these plants is by means of an overhead spray, either with a fine rose attached to the garden hosepipe, or with a rose on the watering-can. The former method is preferable, as the pressure of the spray over the plants is greater, and this helps to keep them clean. The idea that water should not touch the body of these plants in cultivation is completely false. Visitors to our collection remark upon the snowy white colour of the spines of our white-spined Mammillarias and the white hair and wool of such genera as the Espostoas and Eulychnias (see pp. 82 and 84).

The only possible exception to this advice is that in areas where the water contains a high proportion of temporary hardness a white sediment can form not only on the pots and soil, but on the plants themselves. If this is the case a water-softening device is one answer, or you could collect a quantity of fresh rain water, and use an electric pump to spray your plants with sufficient pressure. As to the quantity of water required for each pot: it should be watered strongly overhead, until it is full of water to the rim and overflowing. This method has been used here very successfully for nearly fifty years.

Pests and diseases The chief pests of cacti and other succulents are:

Mealy-bug: a small white crawling insect, often covered with a white powdery substance, which can easily be seen with the naked eye. The eggs are usually to be found amongst some white wool attached to the plant.

Scale insect: small, limpet-like creatures which are immobile and attach themselves firmly to the epidermis (skin) of the plant. They are usually less than $\frac{1}{16}$ in. (1·5 mm) across.

Red spider: these minute red spiders are just visible to the naked eye if a plant is closely examined. Their presence is usually to be expected if a normal green plant suddenly starts to go grey or pale brown even on the newest growth. Genera particularly prone to attack from this insect are those with a rather soft epidermis such as *Chamaecereus*, certain Coryphanthas, Dolichotheles, etc.

These are the main pests and there are various proprietary brands of insecticides available in the shops today, which are suggested for use on house plants. Some of these are contact sprays; others are of a systemic type. Both kinds are normally mixed with water and applied as a spray or drench, but the systemic kind is absorbed into the juice of the plant, so that when an insect sucks the plant for nourishment it also takes in a small amount of poison and kills itself. Many are of an organo-phosphorus type and can be used on all the genera within this book, with the exception of those within the family Crassulaceae. Some of these foliage-type succulents have to be treated rather more carefully, so do read the instructions thoroughly before going ahead and using them. Such insecticides are dangerous, so *do please read the instructions carefully,* and follow them to the letter, not only for the health of your plants, but also for your own safety. If used correctly, they are a far better way of killing pests than the old-fashioned remedies.

However, it is not always emphasised sufficiently that if the same insecticide is used over and over again, the pests will become immune to it within a few generations. In order to avoid this it is advisable to obtain three different insecticides, making certain that their chemical contents, not just their trade names, are different. These three different insecticides should be used in rotation, so that the pests will not be able to build up a resistance to them. Ideally they should be applied as an overhead drench in the spring, mid-summer and late autumn. We consider that red spider can do more harm in a short time than either of the other two, so be on your guard. If an infestation occurs another insecticide may be needed within a shorter time than usual. However, with regular treatment over the length of the season, you should not have to worry too much.

There are a few diseases which can affect some cacti and other succulent plants, but fortunately these are few. One is a type of black-rot that occurs in certain *Trichocerei*, causing unsightly blemishes, and so far there is no certain cure for it. It rarely kills a plant, and a clean offshoot can usually be removed in the following season to replace the scarred old specimen. There is a similar rot which occurs in the Stapelieae, but this can be almost eradicated by using Chinosol (potassium hydroxyquinoline sulphate) as a preventative spray at intervals during the season. This is a more specialised problem, and we will be pleased to give advice on it by letter.

The same powdered fungicide is also used against damping-off disease which happens during seed raising. An orange rot also occurs, often in certain *Ferocacti* and some Opuntias, and this can cause the loss of a plant. It usually appears too late for anything to be done, but sometimes with newly imported plants it can be detected at the point where the roots have been cut. If so, using a very sharp knife or razor-blade you should cut into the tissue until the rot has all been removed, then leave the plants to dry for two weeks in a warm but slightly shaded position before planting. When these blotches appear in Opuntias they only spoil the beauty of the plant, but with globular cacti orange rot can be fatal.

Propagation by cuttings The majority of cacti and other succulents, assuming they are of a branching type, can be propagated by cuttings and it is an easy matter in most cases to do so. All you need is a very sharp knife, secateurs or a saw for some of the larger cacti. It is better to cut them at a narrow joint if possible, but this is not always essential provided the cutting is left long enough for the cut surface to callus over. The majority of cacti and many of the thicker stemmed Euphorbias should be left to dry for about fourteen days while for most of the other succulents and some of the epiphytic cacti (i.e. *Chiapasia*, *Epiphyllum* and *Zygocactus*, etc.) 7–10 days will be sufficient. In fact there are a few of the narrow jointed and more delicate species for which 3–5 days can be sufficient, but this only applies where they are not particularly succulent. If left too long these species could easily dry up completely. All cuttings should be left in a warm but partially shaded position. They can even be covered up with newspaper if left on the greenhouse bench, provided the cut part is exposed to the air.

Once cuttings are ready for planting they can be put into moist sand, vermiculite or loamalite (perlite), but the majority of species can be planted directly into the sand and humus potting mixture and lightly watered every few days. It is really a matter of choice, and some species which are slow to root from cuttings do benefit from a little bottom heat, supplied by heating cables. The cuttings can be kept in an enclosed environment such as an electric propagator, but this is not really necessary except for a few species that are slow to root. It is important that all planted cuttings are not in direct sun, but under shaded glass in a warm position, and regular mist spraying can be beneficial with some of the smaller kinds, particularly with epiphytic cacti. Many cacti and other succulent plants will throw down roots if they are left on the staging in a dry state, but there are others which need moisture before roots will appear.

Some of the succulent plants can be propagated from their leaves, and this is very easy to do. In certain cases as with such genera as *Adromischus* and *Aeonium* a complete leaf is required, whilst others such as *Gasteria* and *Sansevieria* can be propagated from leaf sections. In both cases the leaves should be dried for 3–7 days, according to their size, before laying them on the soil. The leaf-base of complete leaves should be pushed just into the soil mixture; the leaf sections should be pushed further in. These leaves or part leaves will first root, and then later throw up a new shoot, which will grow into a mature plant. The watering requirements are much the same as for ordinary cuttings. There are a few succulents, not illustrated in this book, which develop tiny plantlets either at the tips of their leaves, or along their edges, and these can be grown on in the same way as the leaves of *Adromischus*.

Propagation from seed It is not possible here to give a detailed account of seed-raising, but the following basic principles are sufficient for some of the easier species. Most cacti seedlings and some of the slower growing succulents are quite minute for their first year, in some cases for two years, and their root systems are small and delicate. Because of this the seed-raising compost has to be very poor (about 90 per cent gritty sand to 10 per cent dusty leafmould or peat) and properly sterilised before use. A mixture such as this looks almost like pure sand, and yet there is sufficient nourishment in it for this purpose. Some of the quicker growing *Cerei* and succulents with a similar growth rate could be grown in a slightly richer medium, but it is best to use the same mixture for all kinds, pricking out the quicker growing ones into a richer compost earlier than the others. If you are sowing named seeds (which are better than mixtures) it is best to use small pots, in fact the tiniest ones you can obtain, or those single pop-out type plastic ice-cube containers. If the ice-cube containers are used some small holes should be made in their bases, so that when they stand in a dish of water they can soak it up through the holes in the bottom.

Having sterilised your seed compost and your pots and prepared some trays containing water and a little Chinosol (potassium hydroxyquinoline sulphate, see p. 12) you are ready to start. A tiny weft of cotton wool should be placed at the bottom of the tiny pot, so that it sticks through the bottom and acts like a wick; then place a little sterilised sand on top of that, followed by the seed compost. Scatter your seeds on the surface, and only just cover them with some coarse sterilised sand. Then place your small pot into the water and Chinosol so that it completely soaks it up, and transfer to a tray containing up to $\frac{1}{4}$ in. (6 mm) of water and Chinosol, under which there is heat sufficient to keep the seeds at about 70 °F (21 °C). The seeds should be covered with wire-netting and paper so that they are almost in the dark.

Most kinds will take up to three weeks to germinate, and even then they should still be fairly well shaded, so that the tiny seedlings are a light green colour. After the seeds have germinated they must not be over-watered. They can be grown like this for the first twelve months in most cases, and when they are pricked out into a finely sifted compost, made up along the lines of our simplified potting compost, very little fertiliser should be added, other-wise the soil can go sour very quickly. The reason for this is that the roots of young plants are small, and cannot take up all the nourishment if the soil is too rich, and they will easily rot off at the base.

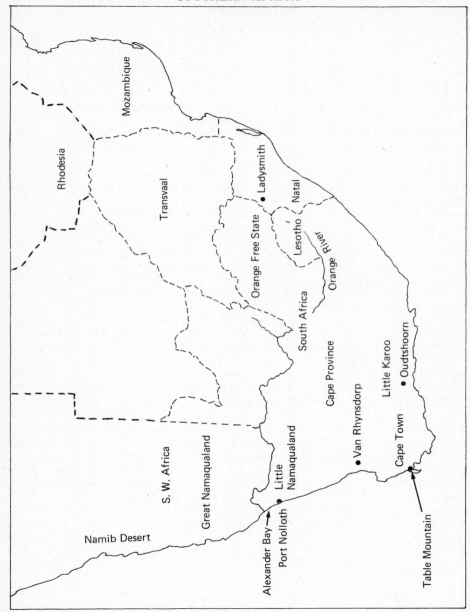

Southern Africa is the home of a very wide range of succulent plants which have adapted successfully to a wide range of climatic conditions.

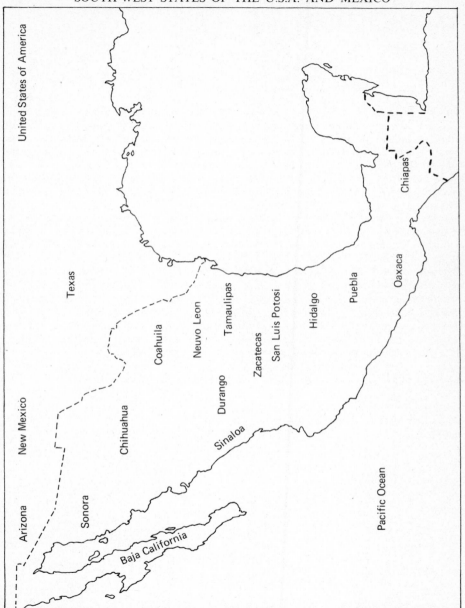

This area is the home of a vast range of cacti. The map shows the states of Mexico where more different species grow than in any other country in the world.

The Exotic Collection

This private botanical garden contains over 9,000 species of cacti and other succulent plants, with five specially laid out greenhouses ranging from our unheated experimental house to other heated ones, including one for the very tropical species. In addition there are rockeries outside for the cacti and other succulent plants which can be grown in the open air throughout the year along with subtropical palm trees and shrubs.

Every month The Exotic Collection sends its subscribers *two new* (previously unpublished) *photographic reference plates in colour*. Size $8\frac{1}{2} \times 6$ in. (23×15 cm), with non-technical cultural notes, etc.

An eight page Monthly Notes (also illustrated in *colour*). A total for one year of 24 plates and 96 pages of Monthly Notes – minimum 72 pages of *full colour*, together with articles and other cultural information. Some of these colour illustrations will cover two pages filmed by us here in the collection or in habitat.

Overseas subscribers also receive an additional 4-page Overseas Newsletter, containing specialised cultural information for varying countries, and this is usually issued bi-monthly.

All subscribers receive a seeds list of named species, some of which are free. Plants also available to subscribers, as well as Chinosol, special cactus fertiliser and sterilised seed soil.

Subscription operates from January to December each year. If you join during any year you will automatically receive all the back issues for the current year to the month of joining. After that future issues will be posted during the first week of each month.

Subscription for one year – £2·50 for the UK and Ireland.

Subscription for one year – $6·50 (USA) or equivalent for all overseas countries.

Under the personal direction of Edgar Lamb and Brian M. Lamb.

Letters to
16, Franklin Road,
WORTHING, Sussex,
BN13 2PQ, England.

Aztekium ritteri Bdkr. $\times 1\frac{1}{2}$
atstekium ritere
Family: Cactaceae

Habitat This species is found in shale cliff areas in the Nuevo Leon part of Mexico.

Description *A. ritteri* was first described by Boedeker in 1929 under the generic heading *Aztekium*, having been previously described by him a year earlier under *Echinocactus*. It is a freely clustering, small growing species, of quite slow growth, with very distinctive horizontal furrows across the ribbed formation of each head. There can be from 9 to 11 ribs, which are invariably in a slightly spiral formation. The areoles are set very close together along these ribs, bearing white hairs rather than spines. Tiny flattened spines do appear for a short time, but soon disappear. The flowers appear from the centre of each head, varying from white to pink, and less than $\frac{1}{3}$ in. (1 cm) in diameter. These appear in profusion in late June or early July and again in August, usually with a gap of a month between the two flowering periods.

Cultivation *A. ritteri* is a fairly slow growing species, and requires a sandy humus soil mixture. It should be grown under lightly shaded glass for best results and should be watered fairly freely during hot weather only. At other times water with care, and we would suggest using a clay pot rather than plastic.

Footnote The specimen illustrated has been in The Exotic Collection for over forty years, and we estimate the age of this plant at about seventy years.

Adromischus pulchellus P.C.H. ×2

adromiskus poolchelus

Family: Crassulaceae

Habitat This genus is native to most parts of South Africa, with many species occurring within Cape Province, whilst some others are also to be found in South West Africa. They are to be found in rock chinks, in sandy soils, often in partial shade under bushes, from sea-level to mountain slopes up to the level where slight frosts can occur.

Description All species within this genus are dwarf in habit, usually up to about 2 in. (5 cm) in height, occasionally less, whilst the largest is *A. grandiflorus*, up to 6 in. (15 cm). Most species have very short stems, bearing a number of very fat succulent leaves in an alternating pattern. The stems are freely clustering, eventually growing into quite large spreading clumps. The leaves vary from ½ to 3 in. (1·25–7·5 cm) in length, in many shapes. They may be flattened or cylindrical tapering to a point, almost egg-shaped or blunt with a wavy edge. The leaves may be smooth, rough or slightly velvety, e.g. *A. schoenlandii*, and are coloured in varying shades of green, purplish green or chalky grey. They are plain or irregularly spotted. The flowers, which are tubular, with 5 small petals opening out slightly at the tip, are rarely more than ½ in. (1·25 cm) long and are white or pink, occasionally purple in colour, with a very short stalk. They are borne on a thin upright or somewhat lax flower spike which is anything from 3 to 10 in. (7·5–25 cm) in length.

Cultivation All species without exception are very easy plants to grow, although some species are slower growing than others. They do well in a sand and humus mixture of about equal parts, with moderate watering from spring to autumn, and should be left completely dry in winter when they are quite safe down to 40 °F (5 °C). They grow equally well on the floor of the greenhouse in pots or on the staging, except that in brighter light the colours of the mottled leaved species may be more brilliant. Oddly enough compared with other members of the family Crassulaceae these plants are rarely troubled by pests such as mealy-bug.

Footnote Most members of this genus make ideal house plants; many of them are quite suited for use in bowl gardens, because of their dwarf habit and unusual mottled leaves, some of which could almost be compared with the mottling on many wild birds' eggs. They can be propagated by cutting or by leaves. If the latter method is used they need only be left to dry for 2–3 days; then lay them on or push them into a sandy humus compost, water them, and within a week or so they will be rooted. After about a month or less a small new rosette will appear from soil level, which will grow to mature size in about six months.

Aeonium arboreum Webb & Berth. $\times \frac{1}{2}$

eonium ahborium

Family: Crassulaceae

Habitat Aeoniums are native to the Canary Islands as well as the Cape Verde Islands and the island of Madeira, whilst *A. arboreum* comes from nearby Morocco. Some species, including *A. leucoblepharum*, appear in east Africa in Somalia. Aeoniums grow from sea-level to above 6,000 ft (1,800 m); one species, *A. smithii*, grows up to 9,000 ft (2,750 m).

Description In general appearance Aeoniums can be divided into three basic groups: species with stemless rosettes and single stemmed kinds, both of which die after flowering, and freely branching shrubby species which can vary from less than 6 in. (15 cm) to over 3 ft (1 m) in height. The rosettes can vary in leaf count from as few as 10 or 12 to between 100 and 200 (in the stemless species *A. tabulaeforme*) and they can be from 1 in. (2·5 cm) to 3 ft (1 m) across. The leaves vary in size and shape considerably depending on the species. They have smooth or velvety surfaces, varying degrees of fleshiness (or succulence), and many have ciliate margins. The leaves come in all shades of green, but many have purplish fleck markings, particularly on the lower surfaces of some species. A few species have pinkish tinged leaves when grown in full sun, e.g. *A. haworthii*. The flowers are in loose or dense rosettes, some bearing as few as 10 or so flowers, others with 100–300. They are usually yellow, but white and pink also occur. The flowers are small, usually around $\frac{1}{4}$ in. (6 mm) across, and there are 6–12 fairly narrow and pointed petals.

Cultivation Aeoniums are very easy plants to grow, and many species come from the cooler valleys in the Canary Islands, where the temperature rarely exceeds 80 °F (26 °C). We have found that most species, particularly stemless rosette kinds and the larger growing free-branching shrub types, do very well when planted out of their pots into the garden in full sun positions for the frost-free months. Their roots are fibrous, so they can be trimmed back if necessary in the late autumn, so that they can return to the same size pot from which they came in the spring. Outside, whether the summer is wet or dry, they develop very healthy large rosettes and as a result flower far more freely during the winter months, when species such as the one illustrated will bloom for 8–12 weeks. These rosettes on the larger shrubby kinds can be from 1 to 2 ft (30–60 cm) in height above the plant. In nature they are winter growers, but fortunately they will change their growing season readily. During the winter months some water should be given, so a minimum of 45 °F (8 °C) is preferable.

Footnote Aeoniums in general are ideal for the person taking up this hobby, as many mistakes can be made regarding culture, but the plants usually survive. If kept in a green-house during the summer when temperatures can exceed 110 °F (43 °C) these plants are prone to attack from ordinary garden pests such as green-fly and black-fly, hence our advice to grow them in the garden. The stemless species, particularly the solitary ones like *A. tabulaeforme*, die when they flower, so can only be propagated from seed or leaf cuttings.

Agave americana fa. variegata Hort. $\times \frac{1}{10}$

(This form is sometimes listed as *A. americana* var. *marginata* Trel.)

agahvi amerikahna (forma) varigahta

Family: Agavaceae (formerly Amaryllidaceae)

Habitat This genus is native only to the Americas (New World) from as far north as Utah and Nevada in the U.S.A., southwards throughout Mexico and most of the other Central American countries, also through much of the West Indies, and the northern part of South America. It is to be found from sea-level, sometimes within spray range of the sea, up to 10,000 ft (3,000 m).

Description Agaves are stemless plants, solitary or clustering, many of them growing quite large, with very strong succulent (fleshy) leaves, usually armed with strong teeth along the margins, and sharp points at the tips. Amongst the smaller growing species is *A. utahensis* with leaves about 4–5 in. (10–12·5 cm) long, whilst the species illustrated, which is one of the larger growing ones, has leaves up to 9 ft (2·7 m) long. The leaf shape can vary too from the type illustrated to others with very narrow leaves, such as *A. stricta*, where the width is much less than $\frac{1}{2}$ in. (1·25 cm). The leaves can vary from shades of green or bluish green, plain and having sharp brown teeth along the margins, to others which have creamy-white markings (as with *A. victoria-reginae*) and just a rough leaf edge. *A. parviflora* is similarly marked but has white threads along the leaf margins. There are a few soft-leaved species, without teeth on the margins or a sharp point. The flowers are somewhat funnel-shaped with a short tube and 6 petals. They are rather dull, often in shades of greenish yellow, occasionally orange, from $\frac{1}{2}$ to 2 in. (1·25–5 cm) long. The flowers come usually in clusters, on short side branches from the main flower spike. This is referred to as a terminal flower scape because the rosette elongates into the flower spike as it does in Aeoniums and Sempervivums. With the smaller species this spike will be only 4–6 ft (1·2–1·8 m) high but it can be as much as 24 ft (7·3 m) in the species illustrated or even as much as 36 ft (11 m) as in *A. franzosinii*. These flower spikes develop quite quickly over a period of a month or so like tremendous telegraph poles.

Cultivation Agaves are exceedingly easy plants to grow; the majority are capable of standing quite cool conditions in winter, down to or even below freezing. Only the West Indian and some of the Central American species require a minimum winter temperature of 45 °F (8 °C). They will grow in any reasonable soil, requiring plenty of water from spring to autumn under shaded glass as young plants, and then full sun conditions in most cases. We have quite a variety of species under cold greenhouse conditions where temperatures have fallen to 16 °F (−9 °C) for a period, whilst we have other specimens, including the one illustrated, growing in the garden. As winter approaches a temporary plastic structure is erected over them to keep the wet from them but they are not heated. There are a few species which can be grown in the British climate outside, completely unprotected provided the soil is very well drained, such as *A. parryi* and *A. utahensis*.

Footnote Agaves in the main are not suited for use as house plants, although very easy to grow, because of the sometimes vicious teeth or points to their leaves. One word of advice for those with children; carefully clip the points off the leaves, to avoid serious eye damage if a child fell on one.

Common Name Century Plant.

Aloe woolliana Pole Evans × Aloe arborescens Mill. ×2

alo wooliana (hybrid) alo ahborescens
Family: Liliaceae

Habitat This genus is native to almost all parts of Africa, Arabia and most of the islands around Africa, including Madagascar. They can be found from sea-level to 8,000 ft (2,666 m). *A. polyphylla* is a native of Phurumela Mountain in Lesotho (formerly Basutoland), where it may be snow covered in winter. They are to be found in very dry desert regions, e.g. *A. pillansii* from the Namib Desert, whilst others grow in dense jungle-like locations in tropical Africa.

Description This genus can be very varied in habit. It includes some stemless clustering species and miniatures which lose most if not all of their leaves during the resting period and resemble Kniphofias ('Red Hot Poker', a well known garden plant also belonging to the family Liliaceae). The larger members of this genus can either grow as dense thickets, e.g. slimmer stemmed species such as *A. ciliaris* and *A. tenuior*, or become truly tree-like, e.g. the solitary *A. ferox* (up to 25 ft, 7·6 m) and multi-branched, e.g. *A. dichotoma* which is of a similar height. All Aloes have fairly fleshy leaves. They are usually in the form of a circular rosette, the exception being species such as *A. haemanthifolia* where the leaves forming the rosette are arranged in one plane. The number of leaves per rosette varies from 6 or 8 in some of the smaller species up to 50 or more. The leaf length varies from less than 1 in. (2·5 cm) in *A. rauhii* to as much as 4 ft (1·2 m) in *A. vaombe*. The leaves are invariably concave to some degree on the upper surface and distinctly convex on the lower. They taper to a pointed tip, sometimes with teeth along the edges as in *A. ferox* with thorns on the upper and lower leaf surfaces. Usually the leaves in varying shades of green are smooth, plain or spotted with paler colours like cream, or they may be striped, e.g. the very well known *A. variegata*. The flowers are tubular, 6 lobed, somewhat angular, from $\frac{1}{3}$ to 1 in. (0·60–2·5 cm) long, sometimes swollen at the base, and are of many colours from pastel hues to vivid orange or red. They are produced as an unbranched or multi-branched inflorescence, usually standing erect, sometimes pendant and from 3 in. (7·5 cm) to 3 ft (1 m) or more in length.

Cultivation Most species of Aloes are extremely easy to grow, and will manage in any reasonable soil. However, the South African species which are most well known will be safe down to 40 °F (5 °C) in winter in most cases, provided they are dry. During the growing season they require plenty of water from spring to autumn, and small or miniature species which show signs of flowering in the winter season in the northern hemisphere should be kept at a slightly higher temperature and watered occasionally. Some of the tropical African species require a minimum of 50 °F (10 °C) in winter, but can still be kept dry. Aloes are easily raised from seed, and even some of the larger species make most attractive and easily cared for plants in their early years. They are quite suited to household conditions, provided they have a reasonable amount of light. Most Aloes (not quite all) can also be rooted from cuttings quite easily, provided they have been dried for 7–14 days, the longer period being required only for a cut end with a diameter of 1 in. (2·5 cm) or more.

Footnote It is possible by careful selection of species to have some member of this genus in flower all the year round! Most of the South African species change their growing and flowering season to suit our seasons in the northern hemisphere.

Aloinopsis rosulata Schwant. ×3

aloinopsis rozulahtus
Family: Ficoidaceae

Habitat This genus is native to the Karoo region in Cape Province, South Africa, growing in stony ground and on rocky slopes, sometimes in association with other members of the family Ficoidaceae such as the genus *Gibbaeum*.

Description They are dwarf clustering plants, usually developing a long tuberous tap-root. Each rosette consists of some 4–10 fleshy leaves in varying shades of green or blue-green. The leaves are often keeled on the under surface and spotted all over. Some species have raised tuberculate spots all over the leaves, whereas others remain completely smooth, e.g. the species illustrated. The fleshy succulent leaves are $\frac{1}{2}$–$1\frac{1}{2}$ in. (1·25–3·8 cm) long and almost 1 in. (2·5 cm) wide. The leaves are widest towards the tip; in addition some are very narrow towards the base and this type is referred to as broadly spathulate. The flowers which vary from $\frac{1}{2}$ to $1\frac{1}{4}$ in. (1·25–3·2 cm) in diameter vary from yellow or salmon to shades of pink, often with a darker median stripe on each petal as shown in the illustration. The flowers are very distinctive for the way in which the stamens remain closely surrounding the pistil. They rarely open before late afternoon, closing again during the evening or after it is dark, and last from 5 to 8 days.

Cultivation These plants are easily raised from seed and most species can reach flowering size within three years. They require a sandy humus soil mixture, should never be over-watered, and because of their deep root system need either a deep pot, or better still, free root-run conditions. Their roots prefer to be cool, so they should not be grown on a top shelf in a greenhouse too near the glass. We grow them under lightly shaded glass with excellent results, under free root-run conditions, and the species shown flowers regularly from early October almost until December – in other words late autumn to nearly mid-winter. In the spring a little water only should be given. This can be increased for the summer and autumn period. In the winter they should be left dry and they will be quite safe down to 40 °F (5 °C) or even a little lower, as in their wild state frosts are not unknown during the winter.

Footnote There is still some difference of opinion among experts, and as a result certain species of *Nananthus* are also listed under *Aloinopsis*. They are most certainly closely related, and require the same cultural treatment. The genus *Aloinopsis* is one of many genera which are commonly referred to as 'stemless *Mesembryanthemae*'. Originally the genus *Mesembryanthemum* was erected by Linnaeus in 1754 to include species which today have been divided up into numerous other genera for a more simple means of classification.

Aporocactus flagelliformis Lem. ×2½

aporokaktus flageliformis

Family: Cactaceae

Habitat Species within this genus are to be found usually in Mexico, where it grows amongst rocks, sometimes in quite moist areas, but also as an epiphyte up in the trees. In the latter instance it grows in the fork of a tree in rotted leaves.

Description *Aporocacti* are slender vine-like cacti, with clambering or pendant spiny cylindrical stems, sometimes up to 6 ft (2 m) in length. The stems, ⅓–1 in. (0·8–2·5 cm) in diameter, are usually bright green. The stems have 10–14 narrow rounded ribs and 10–20 short fine spines at each areole. The flowers are reminiscent of the shape of a coffee-pot spout and are termed 'zygomorphic' because of this unusual shape. They are up to 3 in. (7·5 cm) in length and, depending on the species, vary from pink to carmine or even magenta, and usually appear in the spring. The small globular fruit is covered with bristly spines, rather like those on the plant itself.

Cultivation The species illustrated, of which only a small part of a large specimen is shown, has been in cultivation for the best part of a century, and is as well known as some other epiphytic cacti such as *Zygocactus* (Christmas Cactus) and *Schlumbergera* (Easter Cactus). These species make ideal basket plants, and enjoy a soil rich in humus (leafmould or sedge-peat). Ideally a mixture of 4 parts humus to 1 of gritty sand (by volume) plus a fertiliser which contains bonemeal should be used. They require plenty of water from spring to autumn, when they should be grown under lightly shaded glass and a humid atmosphere can be beneficial. In winter they can be treated in two ways, but the best results are obtained with a minimum temperature of 50 °F (10 °C). A little water can be given, sufficient to prevent the stems shrivelling, or 'die back' occurring at the tips of the stems. They will winter at quite low temperatures, even down to freezing if they are kept dry, but the beauty of the plants will suffer and far fewer flowers will be produced in the following spring. These plants are prone to attack from such pests as red spider and mealy-bug, so a sharp look-out should be kept for them. They also grow exceptionally well, when grafted on to a large *Opuntia* pad or stem of a species of *Cereus*. Specimens grown in this way are often seen in botanical gardens, when the *Aporocacti* tend to become much thicker than usual, but produce an even greater abundance of flowers than they normally do on their own roots.

Common Name Rat's-tail Cactus.

Argyroderma ovale L. Bol. ×3

ahgiroderma ovahli

Family: Ficoidaceae

Habitat Members of this genus are to be found in Cape Province, South Africa within a region south of the Orange River known as Little Namaqualand. Further south they grow in the Karoo desert area, many species being found in the Van Rhynsdorp Division. They grow in stony and sandy soils, sometimes partially buried by sand during the hot dry months.

Description Argyrodermas are dwarf clustering plants, with each rosette or head made up of 2–4 very fleshy succulent leaves, which vary from an almost chalky green to a grey-green colour and are completely smooth without any markings. The leaves can vary in shape from the kind illustrated to some of a semi-cylindrical shape, e.g. *A. braunsii*. In each pair of leaves the surfaces facing each other are flat; the solitary flower bud appears between them. These flowers either have a short stalk or are sessile (no stalk). The flower itself opens wide during the afternoon and early evening, varying in colour from white or yellow to pink and purplish red, from $\frac{1}{2}$ to $1\frac{1}{4}$ in. (1·25–3·2 cm) across and lasting for several days. The normal flowering period in the northern hemisphere is autumn to early winter.

Cultivation They are easy growing plants, fairly free-flowering and not at all difficult to raise from seed, and they can be expected to flower within 3–4 years. As with *Aloinopsis* they need a sandy humus soil mixture, but they differ in having an ordinary fibrous root system, so that a shallower pot can be used. They grow well under lightly shaded glass, but are best left dry for the winter, when a minimum temperature of 45 °F (8 °C) is quite safe, and also for the early part of our spring even though temperatures in a greenhouse can get quite high. Watering should continue from late spring to late autumn or early winter to ensure that the later flowering species produce their fine blooms. These plants are not quick growing, and it is very easy to over-water them and cause unsightly splits to appear within a few hours. If this does happen, the splits will heal and are unlikely to kill a plant.

Footnote This genus contains a great many names but the number of truly distinct species is far fewer than the fifty which have been described. However, they are very suitable for the amateur to grow, as it is possible to grow a variety of them within a small area. Members of this genus and many others within the 'stemless *Mesembryanthemum*' group do well if grown together as a mixture of species in a wide pan.

Common Name Stone Plant.

Ariocarpus kotschoubeyanus K. Sch. ×2½

ariokahpus kotschubianus
Family: Cactaceae

Habitat Members of this genus are native mainly to the northern and central regions of Mexico from Coahuila to Nuevo Leon, and are also found in the southern counties of Texas north of the Rio Grande. They grow in stony and rocky ground, sometimes in sandy clay or often in limestone soil.

Description They are mostly fairly dwarf growing plants, often with a large tap-root and in nature they grow with only their top surface showing above the ground. They are strongly tubercled plants. The tubercles are in some cases long, triangular and smooth, whilst others are flattened with an imbricated upper surface. The areoles are on the tips of the tubercles, but no members of this genus have any spines. The axils between the tubercles are usually full of white wool, and it is from these positions, but near the centre, that the flowers appear. Unlike most other cacti they flower in the autumn, sometimes as late as November in the northern hemisphere. The flowers are funnel-shaped, varying in colour from white or cream to pink and carmine, and 1–2 in. (2·5–5 cm) in diameter. They close at night like most cacti blooms, but last from 3 to 7 days. The fruit, which is somewhat cylindrical, is cream coloured or pale pink when ripe, smooth and fleshy, ½–1 in. (1·25–2·5 cm) long.

Cultivation All members of this genus are slow growing, and although in nature only the top surface is visible above the ground, in cultivation they should be raised slightly above soil level as shown in the illustration. They require a rather sandy humus soil mixture, that is about 2 parts of gritty sand to 1 of humus, and we would recommend the use of a clay pot rather than a plastic one. If only plastic is available an even more porous soil mixture should be used. These plants should always be watered with care and in dull cool weather from spring to autumn none should be given. As with any other cactus plant which requires careful watering, select a hot day and give it a good overhead drench. Provided the soil is sufficiently porous this will do no harm. They can be grown and flowered equally success-fully under lightly shaded glass or in full sun, although we favour the former method. In the winter, provided they are kept dry, a minimum temperature of 45 °F (8 °C) is recommended, or even lower for such species as *A. fissuratus, A. lloydii* and the one illustrated.

Footnote You will also sometimes see the generic name *Roseocactus*, but such plants really belong under the heading *Ariocarpus*. As these plants are so slow growing, it is almost a lifetime's work to grow a reasonably sized plant from seed, so most amateurs purchase young plants 1–2 in. (2·5–5 cm) in diameter which have just reached flowering size.

Common Name Living Rock Cactus.

Astrophytum capricorne B. & R. $\times 1\frac{1}{2}$

astrofetum kaprikorni

Family: Cactaceae

Habitat Astrophytums are native to central and northern Mexico over quite a widespread area up to an altitude of 7,000 ft (2,133 m), although usually much lower. One species, *A. asterias* is also to be found just over the Rio Grande which divides Mexico from the U.S.A., in the south-east corner of Texas in Starr and Hidalgo counties. Plants are usually to be found growing beneath other xerophytic bushes, and this is particularly true of *A. asterias* which is green bodied and completely spineless. They usually grow in rather stony or sandy soil, but *A. asterias* in its eastern range endures at times heavy rain and resulting high humidity, which can certainly not be repeated in cultivation for successful culture.

Description The members of this genus were originally collectively grouped under *Echinocactus*, but Lemaire erected the genus name *Astrophytum* in 1839, referring to the 'star-like structure or formation' of the spineless species, *A. myriostigma*. There are four species within this genus – two spiny and two spineless. All Astrophytums are fairly dwarf globular plants with 4–8 ribs, *A. asterias* possessing rounded ribs, whilst the others are acute. The body surface in some cases has rough mealy-white markings, visible on the species illustrated, in varying degrees of density according to the species or variety. The areoles are well apart in all four species and are fairly woolly in all cases. The two spiny species have quite different types of spines. *A. ornatum* has between 5 and 11 fairly stiff, rounded, erect, yellowish spines up to $1\frac{1}{2}$ in. (3·8 cm) long whilst *A. capricorne* and its varieties have a similar number, but they are flat and weak and almost of a papery texture in shades of black and grey, 1–2 in. (2·5–5 cm) long. All the flowers are funnel-shaped, but opening very wide, yellow, sometimes with an orange-red centre, 2–3 in. (5–7·5 cm) in diameter. The globular fruits, about 1 in. (2·5 cm) in diameter, are densely covered with grey to black short spines, but rather more woolly than spiny in the spineless bodied species.

Cultivation As they are invariably solitary plants they have to be grown from seed, but flowering plants can be produced in 4–5 years, or even less in tropical climates. The seeds germinate quite rapidly and within a few weeks the seedlings are somewhat larger than most other globular cacti at the same age, and one is tempted to give them extra water to hurry them along, but this should not be done, as it can be fatal. We find that all Astrophytums grow well in a slightly sandy humus soil mixture. Grow them under lightly shaded glass and give them plenty of water in very hot weather during the spring to autumn period once the plants are past the $1\frac{1}{2}$–2 in. (3·8–5 cm) diameter stage. Up to three years of age great care must be taken as regards watering, although *A. myriostigma* is without doubt the easiest growing species of all. In the winter, provided they are kept dry, a minimum temperature of 45 °F (8 °C) is sufficient, although *A. myriostigma* will safely stand lower temperatures without harm. *A. myriostigma* var. *nuda* is the exception, preferring a minimum of 50 °F (10 °C) to prevent orange spots developing if the winter humidity is high.

Footnote Astrophytums produce their flowers singly, or sometimes two or three together over a long period from mid-summer to late autumn. *Astrophytum* seeds are very fragile, compared with most other cacti seeds, so they should be handled carefully to prevent crushing.

Common Name Bishop's Hat.

34

Borzicactus humboldtii B. & R. ×1½

borzikaktus humboltie

Family: Cactaceae

Habitat *Borzicacti* are chiefly native to Bolivia, Peru and Ecuador, and are to be found in quite varied locations, from near sea-level to as high as 7,000 ft (2,133 m), growing in well drained places on the slopes or in the valleys. Some species have a widespread distribution from low to high altitudes, resulting in vegetative differences even within a species. The same can be observed in other genera where a species has a distribution over 1,000–3,000 miles.

Description *Borzicacti* are columnar cacti, usually branching at the base, but only remaining erect for their first few years at the most, and then tending to sprawl. The stems, although rather weak, may have a diameter of 2 in. (5 cm) or more, and grow to a length of 4–5 ft (1·2–1·5 m) eventually. There are from 8 to 12 ribs which are low and rounded, with a horizontal cross-groove between the areole positions which are slightly raised on the rib. The areoles are oval with white-brown wool, and up to 1 in. (2·5 cm) apart. Spines are usually clearly divisible between radials and centrals with up to 16 radials, spreading, up to 1 in. (2·5 cm) long, cream to brown in colour. The centrals of which there are rarely more than 4, and often less stand out from the stem and are 1–2 in. (2·5–5 cm) long, and the same colour as the radials. The flowers which last for two days are tubular but opening at the tip in various degrees according to the species. The species illustrated is one of those which does not open to any extent. Most flowers show zygomorphic tendencies to varying degrees (i.e. they are only symmetrical in one longitudinal direction). This is particularly noticeable in *Cleistocactus wendlandiorum* (p. 52) which is very zygomorphic (shaped like the spout of a coffee pot). Fruit is small and round with hairs or bristly spines.

Cultivation *Borzicacti* are easy plants to grow, and even before they reach flowering size they are attractive. They enjoy a soil of about equal parts sand and humus, and plenty of water during the hotter months from spring to autumn. If pot grown, the pot should be as large as the staging space will allow, but the best results of all are obtained by growing under free root-run conditions. All our species are growing in a south facing lean-to greenhouse where they receive all the sun possible, as it is not shaded artificially in any way. However, plants up to 4 or 5 years of age need some protection from the sun. During the winter, provided they are dry, a winter minimum temperature of 45 °F (8 °C) is sufficient.

Footnote There is still considerable controversy as to what species belong under this generic heading. Some authorities consider that the following genera: *Bolivicereus*; *Clistanthocereus*; *Loxanthocereus*; *Maritimocereus*; and *Seticereus* belong here.

Brachystelma barberiae Harv. $\times 1\frac{1}{2}$

brakistelma bahberie

Family: Asclepiadaceae

Habitat Brachystelmas are to be found over a very wide area from Ethiopia to South Africa and in West Africa. Some species which are not very succulent grow in much more humid regions, otherwise they are to be found amongst grass, beneath shrubs in sandy soils.

Description The succulent members of this genus usually possess a swollen tuberous root system, somewhat flattened, with roots on the under-side only and up to as much as 12 in. (30 cm) in diameter as in the species illustrated. These succulent tubers grow in nature with the top surface just visible, or covered with sandy soil during the dormant season when it is very hot. The leaf-bearing stems may stand erect above the tuber but many species produce weak stems which twine up nearby bushes for support (as do the majority of Ceropegias, to which they are closely related). These stems bear pairs of leaves, usually somewhat oval in shape, but pointed at the tip. They are not particularly fleshy, if at all, as they only remain on the plant for 6–7 months during the growing season. In some species, including the one opposite, the flowers often appear by themselves, followed by the leaves when they have finished, and yet the same plants are capable of flowering again when in leaf. These species produce their flowers in umbels (clusters) whereas many of the dwarf trailing species produce a single flower from each leaf axil position along the stem. The flowers are very varied, not only in size – from as little as 2 in. (5 cm) in diameter to as much as 4 in. (10 cm) – but also as regards their shape. The species illustrated is one of the kinds in which the corolla lobes (petals) remain joined at the tip, as in many Ceropegias, whereas others open wide like many of the Stapelias. The corolla lobes of Brachystelmas, Ceropegias and Stapelias are fleshy, almost always 5 lobed, plain coloured, spotted or streaked, and such colours as cream and purple often appear in them.

Cultivation Some species of *Brachystelma* are easier to grow than others, but basically they require a sandy humus soil mixture. They should be grown under lightly shaded glass and always watered with care during the spring to autumn growing period. Although the tubers are almost invisible in habitat, it is advisable in cultivation, particularly in temperate climates, to sit the tuber on the soil and surround it with a $\frac{1}{2}$–1 in. (1·25–2·5 cm) layer of coarse sand or grit for good drainage. The winter minimum temperature is rather dependent on the country of origin of the species in question, but the majority are best kept dry for that period at a temperature no lower than 50 °F (10 °C).

Footnote This genus is not very well known in collections as yet, although a few species are now to be seen. Some species such as *B. barberiae* produce a rather offensive odour when in flower, but many of the smaller flowered kinds do not smell.

Cephalocereus palmeri B. & R. ×1

sefaloserius palmere
Family: Cactaceae

Habitat *Cephalocerei* are quite a large group of plants with a widespread distribution from the Keys in Florida, throughout most of the islands in the West Indies, the north-east parts of Mexico, down to Ecuador and the eastern regions of Brazil. The conditions under which they grow are also variable, but many species grow at or near sea-level under warm, moist, conditions, which gives an idea of their cultural requirements. However, species such as *C. hoppenstedtii* and *C. senilis* come from somewhat higher altitudes in Mexico and do not enjoy quite the same degree of humidity.

Description *Cephalocerei* are all columnar, free-branching species, the majority of them growing fairly erect, some up to 30 ft (9 m) high with a width of 12 in. (30 cm). Some develop thick basal trunks, but there are one or two species which tend to sprawl, such as *C. fluminensis*, native to the coastal areas around Rio de Janeiro in Brazil. They are strongly ribbed plants with 7–30 ribs and the areoles are usually set fairly close together and are very woolly. The wool or hair is sometimes quite long and is usually white. The spine count per areole can vary from 10 to 25. Some are radials spreading out against the body of the plant to a certain degree and up to 10 can be termed as centrals. All the spines are fairly fine; they are usually white, grey or brown and 1–3 in. (2·5–7·5 cm) long. When a stem reaches maturity, some of the areoles develop a great deal more hair or wool and this is termed a *pseudocephalium*. Sometimes this occurs on one side of a stem, in other instances all round a stem at a certain level. The flower buds emerge from the wool at areole positions and remain open for just one night. They are usually bell-shaped, but compared with many other cacti the actual petals are very short. Flower colour is variable but usually in pale shades, off-white, pink, pinkish brown, pale yellow, etc. The fruit is globular, 1–2 in. (2·5–5 cm) in diameter and the remains of the flower stay attached. When the fruit is ripe it splits open in various directions almost like a flower, but remains fairly firmly attached to the plant, displaying the small black seeds often scattered in the brilliant purple pith, or fleshy interior.

Cultivation Most *Cephalocerei* are very easy to grow from seed or cuttings, requiring, with only a few exceptions, a soil containing 50 per cent or more humus to sand, with plenty of water from spring to autumn. They should be grown when young under lightly shaded glass. Older plants can grow in full sun, as they have sufficient spine and wool protection of their own. As for *Corryocacti* free root-run conditions are ideal. In winter, however, many of the species are safest at a minimum of 50 °F (10 °C), when they should remain dry. The slower growing species such as *C. hoppenstedtii* and *C. senilis* need better drainage and a little more care with watering, particularly for young plants. These species, however, will stand a lower winter minimum temperature of 45 °F (8 °C) or even lower, provided they are completely dry.

Footnote The generic name *Cephalocereus* is derived from 'kephalos', meaning a head, referring to the hairy or woolly heads which develop on most of these plants once they reach flowering size. *C. senilis* Pfeiff. is one of the very popular species in cultivation. Because of its dense covering of long white hairs it is commonly referred to as the 'Old Man Cactus' or the 'Old Man of Mexico', whence it comes.

Cereus jamacaru fa. monstrosus Hort. ×1½

serius jamakaroo (forma) monstrosus
Family: Cactaceae

Habitat Species within this genus are native to a wide area of South America, particularly the countries on the eastern side of the Andes range of mountains, as well as Curaçao and some of the other West Indian islands, where *C. repandus* is found. They grow from near sea-level to altitudes where frost occurs in winter.

Description *Cerei* are mostly upright growing tree-like plants, freely branching, which can reach as much as 45 ft (13·7 m) in height and a stem diameter of 12 in. (30 cm). There are also a few low growing or even prostrate species which form dense thickets of stems no more than 3 ft (1 m) in length, in contrast to the others which have a tree-like trunk. They are distinctly ribbed plants with 4–7 ribs, some deeply cut so that the ribs are quite narrow, particularly on new stems, whilst others such as *C. aethiops* have rounded ribs. The circular areoles often bearing white or brown wool are 1–2 in. (2·5–5 cm) apart. The spines, usually divided into radials and centrals, range from 3 or 4 to 12 or more and are grey, brown or black in colour, stiff, varying from ¼ to 2½ in. (0·6–6·3 cm) long, standing out from the green or bright bluish stems. The flowers appear from areoles on old or new stems, but not near the growing point. They are quite large, trumpet-shaped, with a long tube with greenish scales on its exterior. These nocturnal flowers in varying shades of greenish white, white or pink can be up to 10 in. (25 cm) long and 4–5 in. (10–12·5 cm) in diameter. The fruits are slightly oval, up to 5 in. (12·5 cm) long and 3 in. (7·5 cm) across, fleshy, with a smooth exterior. They turn a brilliant shade of red when ripe and have a pleasant fruity odour.

Cultivation All the species are of very easy culture, will grow in any reasonable soil, and require plenty of water during the spring to autumn period. They are mostly strong growing plants, and if given a free root-run can grow 1–2 ft (30–60 cm) per year. As pot plants the growth rate will not be so spectacular, and they can virtually be miniaturised (like the Japanese 'Bonsai' trees) if kept in the same pot for many years. As young plants from seed they make ideal house plants, but will eventually become too large, and up to a height of 2 ft (60 cm) they should be grown under lightly shaded glass, to prevent scorching. Old plants develop a more sun-resistant epidermis. In the winter most species, except those from the West Indies or an area with similar climatic conditions, will safely endure temperatures below freezing if dry. This again applies to older plants rather than those only a few years old. Some of our specimens of *C. peruvianus* and *C. caesius* are grown in an unheated greenhouse where temperatures down to 15 °F (−9 °C) have been recorded.

Footnote Our illustration of a monstrous form of *Cereus* is not typical of the normal structure of a *Cereus*, which really compares with that of *Myrtillocactus geometrizans* (p. 126). However, monstrous forms of various cacti as well as cristates are often cultivated for their unusual appearance.

Cerochlamys pachyphylla L. Bol. ×2

seroclamis pakifila

Family: Ficoidaceae

Habitat This monotypic genus (containing just one species) is native to a fairly small area in the Little Karoo desert in Cape Province, South Africa in the area encompassed by such places as Ladysmith and Oudtshoorn, and grows in stony sandy soil or from chinks in limestone rock.

Description It is more or less stemless, solitary or sparingly clustering plant, rarely growing higher than 3–4 in. (7·5–10 cm). It consists of pairs of leaves opposite each other, elongated, almost triangular in cross-section, keeled on the under surface. They are about 2–2½ in. (5–6·2 cm) long and less than 1 in. (1·25 cm) across, from bluish green in colour with tinges of brown or purple if in full sun and have a slightly waxy surface. The flowers are borne in the centre on a stalk from 1 to 1½ in. (2·5–3·75 cm) long, whilst the flower itself is about 1½ in. (3·75 cm) across when fully open. As in most members of the *Mesembryanthemae* the flowers do not open until mid or late afternoon, closing before dusk and lasting for up to a week. In addition to the purplish form illustrated there is also a white one, which erroneously goes under the variety name 'alba'. In fact the flower colour of this easy-flowering plant can be any shade from white to purple, although the latter is more common.

Cultivation Although *C. pachyphylla* comes from much the same area as *Argyroderma ovale*, this plant enjoys in cultivation a rather richer soil, that is about equal parts sand to humus, also a reasonable amount of water from spring to autumn during warm weather. It can be flowered within two years from seed, and is certainly an ideal plant for someone new to the hobby to try. We grow and flower it very freely under lightly shaded glass in free root-run conditions. It has a fibrous root system but if growing it as a pot plant do not use too small a pot.

Footnote If you are contemplating growing some of the *Mesembryanthemae* under free root-run conditions, do try to group together not only species of a genus but plants of similar growth-rate and cultural requirements. The same comment applies when making up bowl gardens, as too many people make the mistake of mixing slow growing species with quick ones.

Chamaecereus silvestrii B. & R. $\times \frac{1}{2}$

kamiserius silvestrie
Family: Cactaceae

Habitat This species is to be found growing amongst bushes in the mountains between Tucuman and Salta in Argentina.

Description *C. silvestrii* is a low growing, prostrate plant, made up of numerous finger-like stems. These stems vary from $\frac{1}{2}$ to 1 in. (1·25–2·5 cm) in diameter, sometimes reaching up to 6 in. (15 cm) in length. Each stem consists of 8–10 ribs bearing areoles which are set close together, bearing very short, fine, white or straw coloured spines. The flowers which appear in the spring and early summer vary from 2 to 3 in. (5–7·5 cm) in diameter and last for two days.

Cultivation A very easy growing species, it will grow in any reasonable soil, but grows best under lightly shaded glass. It enjoys plenty of water from spring to autumn, whilst in winter it is best kept fairly cool, even down to near or below freezing, provided it is completely dry. If it is kept too warm in winter, this will adversely affect its flowering during the following season.

Footnote The body of this plant is very tender, and as a result is very prone to attack from red spider, which can quickly change a healthy, fresh green-bodied plant to a grey-brown one. Plenty of overhead spraying can deter red spider, but a sharp watch for these minute spiders should always be kept.

Common Name Peanut Cactus.

Chiapasia nelsonii B. & R. $\times\frac{1}{2}$

cheapasia nelsonie
Family: Cactaceae

Habitat This is an epiphytic cactus, growing in the trees amongst rotted leaves in the jungle areas of Honduras and the Chiapas region of Mexico.

Description In young plants the flat succulent stems stand erect, but in two years they become pendant, and in large specimens stems can hang down as much as 4 ft (1·2 m). The edges of the stems are slightly crenate (notched), but no spines grow from the areole positions along the edges. In the spring the flowers appear from these areoles. Plants sometimes send forth thin cylindrical stems, from which many more flattened stems appear. Flowers are about 3 in. (7·5 cm) long, in varying shades of pink or carmine.

Cultivation *C. nelsonii*, as an epiphytic cactus, enjoys warm, humid growing conditions under shaded glass. It requires a soil mixture containing at least 3 parts of humus (preferably beech or oak leafmould) to 1 of sand (by volume). It needs plenty of water from spring to autumn, including overhead mist spraying, whilst in winter it should be kept at a temperature no lower than 45 °F (8 °C), and given some water to prevent shrivelling.

Footnote This species is sometimes listed under another generic heading, *Disocactus*, along with a few other species.

Common Name Orchid Cactus.

51

Cleistocactus wendlandiorum Bckbg. ×2
klestokaktus wendlandiorum
Family: Cactaceae

Habitat *Cleistocacti* are native to rocky and hilly regions, from relatively low altitudes to as
high as 7,500 ft (2,300 m) in central Bolivia and Peru, Uruguay, Paraguay and western

Corryocactus ayopayanus Card. ×2
koriokaktus iyopiyanus
Family: Cactaceae

Habitat *Corryocacti* come from Bolivia and Peru, and can thus certainly be termed a high-
altitude genus, as species within it

Conophytum flavum N.E. Br. ×1½
konofetum flavum
Family: Ficoidaceae

Habitat Conophytums are to be found over a very wide area of Cape Province, South Africa,
also northwards across the Orange River in South West Africa.

Description This genus is very varied, very dwarf, usually stemless and freely clustering. The
small succulent heads which are really two united succulent leaves take on many shapes from
spherical (as illustrated) to egg-shaped, almost heart-shaped or truly bi-lobed. The heads
may be less than ⅛ in. (0·3 cm) in diameter, though the bi-lobed kinds may be ½ by 1 in.
(1·25 by 2·5 cm) in area. The surface is usually in shades of green, smooth, plain or spotted,
and the bi-lobed species often have a red edge to the lobes. The flowers appear from the
centre; some open wide as illustrated and are over ½ in. (1·25 cm) across whilst others barely
open and look more like a minute shaving-brush. Their colour can vary from white or cream
to yellow and shades of pink and purple.

Cultivation Most species prefer a sandy humus soil mixture, and as they have a fairly clearly
defined growing season the watering should be as follows. Dry from November to March;
mist spraying or very light watering from April to June; normal overhead watering from
July to October. Grow under lightly shaded glass. In the November to March period a
minimum of 40 °F (5 °C) is quite sufficient for most species.

Footnote In the resting stage the plants shrivel up into the old heads (or leaves) and look
quite dead.

Coryphantha vivipara var. arizonica Mshll. ×1½

korifantha vivipara (variety) arizonika

Family: Cactaceae

Habitat Coryphanthas have a widespread distribution over North America from as far north as Alberta in Canada to the south-western states of the U.S.A. and in Mexico. The conditions under which they grow are very varied: they grow amongst grass and beneath trees in the north, where snow and severe freezing occur in winter, as well as in hot dry areas.

Description Coryphanthas are usually globular plants, solitary or freely clustering. They are mostly strongly tubercled with each tubercle bearing a circular or oval areole carrying 1–10 or more spines. In certain species one or two spines are stouter and hooked. They are rarely more than 1 in. (2·5 cm) long and are very variable in colour. Flowers vary from ½ to 2 in. (1·25–5 cm) in diameter, somewhat funnel-shaped, and in almost any colour except blue, which is not found in any cactus blossom. The outer petals are sometimes ciliate (feathered). Fruits are usually egg-shaped, sometimes as much as 2 in. (5 cm) long, but often less, and quite fleshy, green or red when ripe.

Cultivation Coryphanthas are easy growing plants, enjoying a soil of about equal parts sand and humus. The softer-bodied kinds enjoy plenty of water during the warmer months and should be grown under lightly shaded glass. The harder-bodied kinds where the spines are much stiffer, such as *C. recurvata* or *C. robustispina*, require a sandier compost, and will stand full sun conditions. They should be kept dry in winter down to 40 °F (5 °C), and some even lower than that such as *C. vivipara* and its varieties.

Common Name Beehive Cactus.

Cotyledon orbiculata L. × 1½

kotiledon orbikulahta
Family: Crassulaceae

Habitat This genus is native chiefly to South and South West Africa, but a few other species do exist outside this area as far north as southern Arabia. They grow in quite varied locations in very dry semi-desert regions up to the lower mountain slopes, including Table Mountain near Cape Town in South Africa where *C. grandiflora* lives under quite moist conditions at certain times of the year.

Description They are mostly shrubby free-branching plants, some very dwarf, such as *C. buchholziana* which rarely exceeds 3 in. (7·5 cm) in height compared with *C. wickensii* which can exceed 6 ft (1·8 m). They can be divided basically into two groups: the 'caudiciform' species have weird contorted or knobbly stems and bear plain green leaves when in growth, but are naked in the dry resting season. The slim-stemmed species usually bear leaves that last for two or three years. The first group usually have very swollen stems, which are smooth surfaced or knobbly. This is sometimes caused by the bases of the leaf stalks which remain attached after the leaves have dropped off, e.g. in *C. cacalioides* and *C. wallichii*. Some of these also have a papery bark which peels off periodically as the stems swell with age. The bright green leaves may be flat or cylindrical, and taper to a point up to 3 in. (7·5 cm) long. The other group have slim stems ¼–½ in. (0·6–1·25 cm) thick, brown or grey in colour, which bear heads of leaves that are either plain green with red tips and a chalky surface or green with a velvety surface. The leaf shape can also vary as in the other group. Even in a single species such as *C. orbiculata* tremendous variations occur from one colony to another. The flowers in both groups are very similar in structure. They are produced on a terminal inflorescence, sometimes branched and from 3 to 20 in. (7·5–50 cm) in length. The flowers themselves are pendant, from ½ to 2 in. (1·25–5 cm) long, usually rather tubular with 5 petals. The flowers of the species in the first group tend to be uninspiring white, cream or green, whereas in the second group various shades of pink and purple appear, and the exterior of the tube is often of a similar colour to the leaves of the same plant.

Cultivation Cotyledons are all easy growing plants which will grow in any reasonable soil which does not set too hard. Most species grow best under lightly shaded glass, and require plenty of water during the growing season; however, this is where the two groups differ. The second group grow during the spring to autumn period in the northern hemisphere whereas the others prefer to come into leaf in our autumn, equivalent to the South African spring. This means that a minimum temperature above 45 °F (8 °C) is safest so that they can be watered periodically. The other Cotyledons, however, can be kept at about the same temperature, and to prevent too much leaf fall can be watered very occasionally during autumn. In the summer the deciduous Cotyledons should be given some water in the northern hemisphere, otherwise the plants will shrivel rather too much.

Footnote Although this is not a huge genus it has been difficult to group them other than into deciduous and non-deciduous species. All species make worthy house plants, but as they can become leggy rather easily it often pays to under-water them.

Crassula nealeana Higgins. ×2

krassula neliahna

Family: Crassulaceae

Habitat This genus is a very large one, with the greatest number originating from South Africa, but other species are to be found throughout much of tropical Africa, and as far north as Arabia. A few species are to be found in other parts of the world. They grow in varied locations from desert regions to quite moist mountain slopes.

Description Crassulas are usually freely clustering plants, sometimes erect, occasionally pendant. Some are very dwarf with exceptionally succulent leaves, e.g. *C. cornuta* and its relatives; others are of shrub or even tree-like proportions, e.g. *C. argentea* and *C. arborescens*. However, they all have fleshy leaves in varying degrees of succulence, produced in pairs opposite one another, sometimes crowded together into tight rosettes. The flowers are small, white, cream, pink, etc. made up of ten parts, that is 5 sepals and 5 petals, and are usually produced as a fairly dense inflorescence. This is sometimes in the form illustrated or may be many inches across and made up of 50 or more flowers. Some species are highly scented, and with a careful choice of species, it is possible to have a range of plants which bloom during all months of the year.

Cultivation Generally speaking the majority of species are very easy growing, but when cultivating these plants, it is beneficial to try and find out roughly their country of origin. For example species such as *C. cornuta* and other similar semi-desert types require sandier compost and less than average water, whereas the species illustrated and the tree-like ones mentioned above prefer a richer soil and more water during the spring to autumn period. All the species with the exception of those from tropical Africa will be quite safe in winter down to 40 °F (5 °C) provided they are dry, and this latter requirement is rather more important with the miniatures with very fleshy leaves and tight rosettes. Some of the others such as *C. nealeana* and the shrubby kinds can benefit from a little water occasionally during the winter period. This is particularly true when they are kept at a higher minimum temperature, or used as house plants, for which they are most suited, so as to prevent too much leaf loss. If this happens it will not kill the plant, but it can tend to detract from its beauty if it loses half its leaves, and becomes too leggy. Some species in age will naturally do this, but fortunately most Crassulas are easily propagated from cuttings. All you need to do after taking the cuttings is to leave at least 1 in. (2·5 cm) of stem which can be pushed into the soil mixture, after the cutting has been allowed to callus for about a week. All Crassulas will grow well under lightly shaded glass, but those species with chalky or more brilliantly coloured leaves will take more sun, and can produce more brilliant shades.

Footnote This genus is worthy of a study on its own because of the tremendous variation in form and size. Very many species of Crassulas are ideally suited for use as house plants, and are easily propagated from cuttings in almost all cases.

Common Name Bead Plant.

Denmoza erythrocephala Bgr. $\times \frac{1}{2}$

denmoza erithrosefala

Family: Cactaceae

Habitat Denmozas are native to Argentina, in the region of Mendoza and Tucuman, in scrub-bush areas.

Description Denmozas are solitary and usually globular for the first ten or twenty years, but become cylindrical in age and grow up to 4 ft 6 in. (1·4 m) in height and as much as 12 in. (30 cm) in diameter. The stem consists of up to 30 fairly straight, rounded ribs, bearing areoles which are $\frac{1}{2}$–1 in. (1·25–2·5 cm) apart. Each areole bears up to 30 straight or slightly curved spines, varying from brown to rusty red, rarely exceeding 1 in. (2·5 cm) in length. The tubular flowers appearing from near the centre are about 3 in. (7·5 cm) long, and only open sufficiently for the style and stamens to be exserted. Fruit globular, slightly spiny and hairy, red, about 1 in. (2·5 cm) in diameter.

Cultivation Denmozas are usually raised from seed, and take many years to reach flowering size, but are worth growing for the beauty of their spines. They grow well under lightly shaded glass in a soil of about equal parts sand and humus, with plenty of water during all warm weather from spring to autumn. In winter they are safe down to 40 °F (5 °C) provided they are completely dry.

Footnote The flowering period is very variable from early summer to early autumn, and we have had buds which were produced late in the autumn, remained dormant through the winter and developed in the early spring.

Dolichothele longimamma B. & R. ×1

dolikotheli lonjimamma
Family: Cactaceae

Habitat This genus is native to the south-east part of Texas and northern Mexico, where it usually grows in rather sandy soils, amongst grass and under various xerophytic bushes.

Description Dolichotheles are freely clustering, low growing plants whose roots below ground are often somewhat finger-like and very succulent (fleshy). Each head consists of numerous conical tubercles, with the areole and spine cluster at the tips. The spines are fairly fine, flexible, white or horny yellow. The funnel-shaped flowers usually appear in a ring as in most Mammillarias, from positions between the tubercles. They are in varying shades of yellow and up to 2 in. (5 cm) in diameter, and are highly scented.

Cultivation Dolichotheles are very easy plants to grow and flower. They may be raised either from seed, plant division, or even grown from single tubercles, whereby a new plant will form from the areole position. They enjoy a soil mixture of about equal parts humus and sand, should be grown under partially shaded glass, and because of their large roots a deep pot is preferred. They require plenty of water from spring to autumn, and enjoy a rather more humid atmosphere at this time of year than many other globular cacti. In winter a minimum of 40 °F (5 °C) is quite safe for most species, provided they are completely dry.

Footnote As these plants have a rather soft body they are prone to attack by red spider (see *Chamaecereus silvestrii*, p. 50).

65

Dudleya formosa Moran. ×1½

dudlea formosa
Family: Crassulaceae

Habitat The genus is native chiefly to Mexico, including the Baja California peninsula; it also grows in nearby islands, and northwards in California, Arizona, Nevada and Oregon. They are to be found growing at sea-level on sea-facing cliffs, also at high altitudes in a few cases where light frosts occur, and in such a position that the rosettes do not hold the moisture to any great extent.

Description Dudleyas can be either stemless or short-stemmed, solitary or branching into clumps, with the rosettes bearing numerous fleshy, very succulent leaves. Unlike some other succulent plants of similar formation, the old leaves invariably remain attached to the stem below the rosette, tending to give a somewhat untidy appearance; this is visible in the illustration of *D. formosa*. The leaves can be either somewhat cylindrical, tapering to a point (*D. densiflora*) or, like those in the illustration, green or chalky white in colour. The flowers are produced as an inflorescence, sometimes branched, on a stem which can vary from 3 to 18 in (7·5–45 cm) in height, depending on the species. The flowers, consisting of 5 petals, are campanulate, opening wide with the petals sometimes slightly recurved as illustrated, white, yellow or pink in colour, and some species are slightly scented. They usually appear in late spring and summer.

Cultivation Dudleyas are not so commonly grown as the genus *Echeveria*, to which they are related. The two plants have a somewhat similar habit and grow in many cases under similar conditions, sometimes even side by side. Most species are far from rapid growing, and require a soil of about equal parts sand and humus, with average watering from spring to autumn under lightly shaded glass. They can take full sun treatment in most cases, provided they are not too near the glass to risk leaf burn. In winter a minimum of 40 °F (5 °C) is suitable for most species, provided they are dry, and they lose far fewer leaves than Echeverias at this time of year. Dudleyas are also very suitable as house plants, but this does mean a sunny window-sill position, particularly with the chalky leaved species.

Footnote Some species that come from cooler situations in nature do not enjoy very hot greenhouse conditions during summer, so should be grown at that time in pots on the floor of the greenhouse, where they are not in direct sun. If plants start to lose leaves during the summer period, this is often a guide, if you have been unable to ascertain the habitat conditions for a certain species. They are certainly easy plants to grow, although far from quick growing, and can be grown easily from seed or propagated by cuttings, provided they have been left to callus for about a week prior to planting.

Duvalia modesta N.E. Br. $\times 2\frac{1}{2}$

duvalia modesta

Family: Asclepiadaceae

Habitat Most species within this genus are to be found in the Cape Province area of South Africa, but some occur in South West Africa, Transvaal and Natal, Rhodesia, Mozambique, Kenya and Southern Arabia.

Description Duvalias are dwarf, mostly prostrate growing plants. The majority have somewhat egg-shaped, very succulent jointed stems, green or greenish brown in colour, which average from $\frac{1}{2}$ to 2 in. (1·25–5 cm) in length and $\frac{1}{2}$–$\frac{3}{4}$ in. (1·25–1·9 cm) in diameter at the widest point. The exceptions are *D. polita* which also burrows and has erect slim cylindrical stems up to $2\frac{1}{2}$ in. (6·25 cm) long, and two prostrate growing species, *D. procumbens* and *D. tanganyikensis* where the stems can be up to 6 in. (15 cm) in length. All the species have 4–6 angled, leafless stems. The flowers which appear in the summer and autumn are 5 lobed, and vary from $\frac{1}{2}$ to 1 in. (1·25–2·5 cm) in diameter. They are usually in shades of reddish brown and purple, but one or two are cream coloured. The corolla lobes (petals) are usually folded back slightly. One of the exceptions to this is *D. procumbens*.

Cultivation Duvalias will grow very well in a mixture of about equal parts sand and humus, with average watering from spring to autumn, and should be grown under lightly shaded glass. In winter most species are safe down to 40 °F (5 °C) if they are kept dry. The tropical African species need a temperature not lower than 50 °F (10 °C) and a little water occasionally.

Common Name Carrion Flower.

Echinocactus horizonthalonius Lem. ×1½

ekinokaktus horizontalonius
Family: Cactaceae

Habitat This genus is native to the south-western part of the U.S.A. as well as northern and central Mexico, growing in sandy and rocky hillside locations, in very hot dry situations.

Description *Echinocacti* are globular or cylindrical in habit, solitary or clustering. Many species such as *E. visnaga* and *E. grandis* grow to huge dimensions – as much as 6 ft (1·8 m) in height and 3 ft (1 m) in diameter – but such specimens may be one hundred or more years old. *Echinocacti* have a prominent rib structure, a very tough epidermis (outer surface) enabling them to withstand full desert sun conditions, and large areole positions at intervals along the ribs. The areole position is usually very woolly on the newer ribs in the centre, whilst the spines are normally straight or slightly curved, very strong, and in some species up to 2 in. (5 cm) or more in length. These either lie against the body or stand erect away from the plant. They are very variable in colour. Flowers are rarely more than 2½ in. (6·25 cm) in diameter, yellow or sometimes pink or reddish. Fruit is scaly and woolly, often highly coloured.

Cultivation Most species are easy to grow. The species illustrated requires a rather more sandy soil mixture than the others, which will grow well in a mixture of about equal parts gritty sand and humus. They need average water from spring to autumn, but none in winter when a minimum temperature of 40 °F (5 °C) is advisable, and they should be kept completely dry. Young plants are best grown under shaded glass.

Common Names Blue Barrel Cactus, Eagle's Claw.

Echeveria pulvinata Rose. ×2
ekiveria poolvinahta
Family: Crassulaceae

Habitat The genus centres on Mexico and some of the countries to the south in Central America, whilst a few species are to be found in various parts of South America, and one or two to the north in the U.S.A. They are to be found from sea-level up to the mountains, where some species can endure light frosts.

Descriptions Echeverias can be either stemless, solitary or clumping or may grow as low, fairly freely branching shrubs. The fleshy leaves are arranged spirally in rosettes which may be slightly cylindrical or flattish in shape and which end in a point. The leaves, which may be smooth or velvety as in the illustration, are 1–12 in. (2·5–30 cm) long and vary in colour from green to blue-grey, pink or purplish red, e.g. *E. gibbiflora* var. *metallica*. The latter colours occur in the species which have a powdery bloom on the leaves, and these species are in the majority. The leaves are never spotted, but some have vivid coloured margins or leaf-tips. The flowers appear as an elongated inflorescence, sometimes branched, and are slightly bell-shaped. These flowers vary from ½ to 1 in. (1·25–2·5 cm) in length and the sepals, like the leaves, often have a velvety texture or a powdery bloom. The petals, which may be yellow, pink, red or occasionally white, are sometimes similar in texture.

Cultivation Echeverias will mostly grow in any reasonable soil, but we have found that our normal mixture of about equal parts sand and humus suits them well. The stemless species such as *E. agavoides*, which is slower growing and possesses a very tight rosette, should be watered a little more carefully, with a good layer of grit or coarse sand around the neck to allow for drainage. The shrubby kinds enjoy more water during the spring and early summer, but in order to develop their brilliant leaf colouring less water should be given from that time until the end of the autumn. They can be grown under lightly shaded glass or full sun, provided they are a few feet from the glass, as occasionally leaves can be burned. In winter most species can go down to below 40 °F (5 °C) with complete safety provided they are dry. However, this means that additional leaves will be lost through dryness, so if you do not want this to happen keep the temperature above 45 °F (8 °C) so that they can be watered occasionally. Every species carries an optimum amount of leaves per rosette, and a number of the lowest leaves dry up each year to be replaced by others.

Footnote Echeverias can easily be propagated by cuttings or even single leaves, as well as by seed. The taller species do become leggy, but it is an easy matter to cut the rosette off with about 1–2 in. (2·5–5 cm) of stem, dry for a week and replant, and it will very quickly re-root. A few species come from higher altitudes, as with Dudleyas, and when grown in the greenhouse these should be placed in their pots on the floor where it is a little cooler in midsummer.

Echinofossulocactus pentacanthus B. & R. ×2

ekinofossulokaktus (stenokaktus) pentakanthus

Family: Cactaceae

Habitat These plants are chiefly native to the eastern parts of Mexico, particularly in the states of Hidalgo and Zacatecas, growing invariably in partial shade beneath bushes, or in some cases almost invisible amongst grass.

Description These plants are small growing, globular or short-cylindrical, solitary or clustering in age, and with the exception of one species, *E. coptonogonus* they have a large number of thin wavy ribs. The number of ribs varies considerably; the species illustrated has about 30 and *E. multicostatus* has as many as 120. The areoles bearing the spine clusters are set quite far apart on the ribs. The radial spines are fine and the few centrals are usually flattened and pressed against the plant. The flowers, which rarely exceed 1 in. (2·5 cm) in diameter vary from white or yellow to pink, often with a median darker stripe on each petal. The fruit is very small, with papery scales on its exterior.

Cultivation All the species are very easy to grow, although not fast growing, but do well in a sand and humus mixture of about equal parts by volume. They need average water from spring to autumn, and should be grown under lightly shaded glass; the less spiny species need a little extra shade during the hottest period of the year. In winter if they are kept dry a minimum temperature of 45 °F (8 °C) is satisfactory.

Footnote Many species in this genus were inaccurately described as *Stenocactus*.

Epiphyllum 'Peacockii' Hort. $\times \frac{1}{2}$
epifilum (hybrid) pekokie
Family: Cactaceae

Habitat Epiphyllums as the name suggests are epiphytic cacti growing in the forks of jungle trees, where there are rotted leaves. They are to be found over a wide area from the jungles of southern Mexico to Panama in Central America and southwards into Brazil; also in some of the islands of the West Indies such as Trinidad and Tobago.

Description Epiphyllums are very similar in habit to *Chiapasia nelsonii* (p. 51), but as a general rule the flat green stems grow rather larger, and the old basal parts of a plant become very woody. The true species found in the wild, unlike the hybrid illustrated, have large white flowers with a rather slender tube, opening at night. Some species have a very unusual stem structure, almost like a skeleton as the stems are deeply notched. *E. oxypetalum* has flowers 10 in. (25 cm) long.

Cultivation These plants, like *Chiapasia nelsonii*, require a soil rich in humus, and much the same treatment is required, but some of the true species are best kept at a winter minimum temperature of 50 °F (10 °C).

Footnote A list of hybrids has not been given, as all of them are worthy of culture. Many brilliant colours have been produced by hybridising *E. ackermannii* and *E. crenatum* with *Nopalxochia phyllanthoides*, *Heliocereus speciosus*, various *Selenicerei* and *Hylocerei*, etc.

Common Name Orchid Cactus.

Echinopsis kermesina Buxbaum. $\times 1\frac{1}{2}$

ekinopsis kermersena

Family: Cactaceae

Habitat Species within this genus are to be found over quite a wide area of South America, particularly in Argentina, Uruguay, Paraguay and southern Brazil, but also in the higher mountain area of Bolivia up to 7,500 ft (2,300 m). Some species grow in sandy areas at low altitudes, but many others are to be found amongst rocks, with other kinds of vegetation, in the mountains of some of those countries.

Description The genus *Echinopsis* was first established by Zuccarini in 1837, so that a few species, or hybrid forms of them, particularly those with the large trumpet flowers, have been in cultivation for a very long time. Most species are globular, but a few in age do become short-cylindric; one or two remain solitary, whilst the majority cluster very freely. Each head is prominently ribbed, usually straight and often raised at the areole positions, almost giving a tubercled appearance. Individual heads can occasionally reach as much as 12 in. (30 cm) in diameter in a few species and up to 3 ft (1 m) in height, but by far the majority attain only half or one third this size. The spination is very variable as regards number and size, but in most cases they stand out from the plant in a fairly erect manner. The large trumpet-shaped flowers, which are white or pink, usually remain open for about twenty-four hours, and these are highly scented. The species with the vividly coloured flowers, such as the one illustrated, open for nearly two 'daylight days'. The largest flowers can reach 10 in. (25m) in length and about one third to one half that in diameter. The flower bud is normally very hairy and the outside of the flower tube has some fine spines and quite a lot of hair. The same sort of covering applies to the globular fruit. The flowering period is in the summer.

Cultivation Almost all species of *Echinopsis* are very easy to grow, but many species grow and flower better under lightly shaded glass, particularly those species which are rather sparsely covered with spines. The species from higher altitudes do not enjoy temperatures too much in excess of 100 °F (38 °C), and prefer to be grown in good-sized pots on the floor of the greenhouse. They enjoy plenty of water from spring through to autumn, and do exceedingly well in a soil containing humus. However, they are mainly very tolerant plants, and will grow reasonably well in almost anything! In the winter most species will be quite safe at temperatures near freezing if they are dry. We have been successfully growing various hybrid forms of *E. multiplex* and *E. eyriesii* in our unheated greenhouse for some twenty-five years.

Footnote *E. kermesina* is also to be found under another generic name – *Pseudolobivia kermesina* Krainz. – but we feel that species of *Pseudolobivia* must belong in the genus *Echinopsis*, in the same way as Mediolobivias are now termed as Rebutias. Many hybrids between *Echinopsis* and *Lobivia* are also in cultivation, many with brilliantly coloured flowers, and these require identical treatment.

Encephalocarpus strobiliformis Bgr. ×3

ensefalokarpus strobiliformis

Family: Cactaceae

Habitat The one and only member of this genus is native to the gravelly hills in the state of Tamaulipas, Mexico. It is almost invisible to the naked eye, except when it gives itself away during the flowering period.

Description The name *Encephalocarpus* was erected by Berger in 1928, to describe one species, previously described as *Ariocarpus strobiliformis* Werd. It is a globular or egg-shaped plant, whereas most *Ariocarpus* have a flat-topped general appearance (see *A. kotschoubeyanus*, p. 32) and it differs from that genus in the following ways. *Encephalocarpus* consists of a head made up of a large number of scale-like tubercles, each with a keel on the under surface, almost like the cone from a coniferous tree. The generic name refers to the inflorescence (flower head) of *Encephalartos*, a member of the family Cycadaceae, which it closely resembles, and the specific name *strobiliformis* is derived from the word 'strobilum' or cone. Each head averages 1½–2½ in. (3·75–6·25 cm) in height and diameter. The axils at the base of each scale-like tubercle bear white wool, and in fact the centre of the plant is quite woolly. The flowers which appear from this central white woolly area are funnel-shaped, up to 1½ in. (3·8 cm) in diameter, sometimes much less than this. The petals are in shades of violet-pink, and the outer ones are slightly fringed. The anthers on the stamens are a brilliant yellow colour in contrast to the petal colour. The fruit is small, dry, and barely visible amongst the scale-like tubercles.

Cultivation This plant requires much the same cultural treatment as *Ariocarpus*. It is, however, easier to raise from seed and plants big enough to flower can be produced in 6–8 years under greenhouse conditions in a temperate climate.

Footnote Specimens of this plant in collections are usually single-headed but in age they form into clusters of a few heads. In the seedling stage for the first year or so minute spines are visible but soon disappear. These are also visible on small newly formed offsets.

Espostoa lanata var. mocupensis Rttr. ×1¼

espostoa lanahta (variety) mokoopensis
Family: Cactaceae

Habitat Espostoas are native to Peru and southern Ecuador, where they are to be found growing on dry hillsides and mountain slopes between 3,000 and 7,500 ft (1,000 and 2,300 m).

Description They are columnar, growing up to 12 ft (3·6 m) or so in height, branching from the sides of the main trunk into further erect stems. The stems are so densely covered with hair and wool that the straight rounded rib structure is often completely obscured (see the illustration, which depicts just the top 8 in. (20 cm) or so of a 3 ft (1 m) high specimen). The stem diameter in age rarely exceeds 4 in. (10 cm), and there can be from 20 to 30 ribs on old stems. The hairy or very woolly areoles are set very close together, bearing up to 12 fine radial spines, white to horny yellow in colour, ½–1 in. (1·25–2·5 cm) long. Central spines are often not present even on plants ten years old, but if they are they will only be 1 in. (2·5 cm) long and sometimes of a different colour (see illustration). In old specimens the central spines can reach as much as 3 in. (7·5 cm) in length. Espostoas produce a true lateral cephalium, that is a mass of hair and wool which forms from areoles usually on one side of the stems. It is from these same areoles that the flowers appear. The flowers are up to 2 in. (5 cm) in diameter, somewhat bell-shaped; the exterior part of the tube is covered with scales and hairs. The nocturnal flowers are usually white. Fruits are slightly oval, like the flower tube, and are up to 1½ in. (3·8 cm) long.

Cultivation Espostoas are normally raised from seed, although cuttings can be rooted off old plants, as with most other cacti of similar growth habit. Seedlings are not too slow growing, but for the first five years or so care should be taken not to over-water them, as they can easily rot off at ground level. They enjoy a soil of a sandy-leafmould nature, and should be grown under lightly shaded glass for the first few years, and watered carefully unless the weather is very hot during the spring to autumn period. In the winter in any climate where the atmospheric humidity can be high, a minimum temperature of 45 °F (8 °C) is safest. In nature the plants stand much lower temperatures but the humidity is very low, and the woolly covering protects the plant from the cold. Older plants can have more water, provided one always ensures that the soil has more or less dried out from the previous time.

Footnote Espostoas are grown by most people for the beauty of the plant because as with a few other columnar cacti, and even the globular *Melocacti* which have cephaliums, specimens will take many years to reach flowering size. We have growing here in The Exotic Collection seed-grown specimens some 3 ft (1 m) in height which are not flowering size, and yet this represents twenty years' work. Admittedly in a more tropical climate with a longer growing season, quicker growth will result, but even then the plant will still take many years to reach flowering size. However, the compensation is the beauty of the plants with their densely woolly appearance.

Euphorbia bevilaniensis Croizat. $\times 1\frac{1}{2}$

uforbia bevilaniensis
Family: Euphorbiaceae

Habitat Succulent members of this genus are to be found in almost all parts of Africa, as well as in the neighbouring islands such as the Canary Islands and Madagascar, in Arabia, India and Sri Lanka (Ceylon). A few others are to be found in the East Indies as well as North, Central and South America. They grow under very varied climatic conditions to which they have adapted themselves.

Description The genus *Euphorbia* has adapted itself to suit all sorts of environments, and like many other genera it includes some species which are succulent and others which are truly non-succulent. Euphorbias have milky sap, like all other genera within the family Euphorbiaceae, including the rubber tree (*Ficus elastica*). They differ in stature to a tremendous degree, varying from less than $\frac{1}{2}$ in. (1·25 cm) in height to as much as 30 ft (9 m), e.g. *E. ingens* and *E. neglecta*. Their succulence can be in the form of a swollen root system bearing succulent or non-succulent leaves (*E. francoisii* and *E. decaryi* fall into the latter category). There is a considerable number of species of tree-like proportions with angled or ribbed stems, similar to many *Cereus* type cacti, with or without leaves on the new growth. In this group *E. canariensis* is leafless, whilst species such as *E. ingens*, *E. candelabrum* and *E. neriifolia* have leaves on the new growths and pairs of short thorns beneath each leaf position. There are also many shrubby species with either smooth cylindrical stems bearing terminal rosettes of non-succulent leaves (e.g. *E. balsamifera* and *E. obtusifolia*), or with thorny stems and non-succulent leaves (see illustration). We can also introduce you to further variations such as the almost spherical species including the well known *E. obesa*, which remains solitary whilst *E. meloformis* is of a clustering habit. Another very distinctive section within the genus *Euphorbia* is the 'caput-medusae' group. These are invariably tap-rooted plants bearing numerous succulent tails of varying thicknesses and lengths, and they are without spines, but are low growing in habit. There are in fact many other intermediate forms too numerous for inclusion here, but all of them have a distinctive 'flower' structure. It is not exactly a true flower, and is technically referred to as a cyathium, sometimes surrounded by a brilliantly coloured pair of cyathophylls as in the illustration. These 'flowers' consist of just the basic parts necessary to produce pollen and seeds. In some cases there are male and female 'flowers' either on the same plant or on different ones (as in *E. obesa*), but when combined in the same 'flower' the female part is in the centre surrounded by a few stamens bearing pollen. The seed pod when formed is a capsule divided into three sections, and when ripe it explodes, often scattering the three small hard seeds many feet (a metre or so) from the parent plant.

Cultivation Most Euphorbias will grow well in a soil mixture of about equal parts humus and sand, with average watering from spring to autumn under lightly shaded glass. The South African and other non-tropical African species can winter at a minimum temperature of 45 °F (8 °C) provided they are kept dry, whereas the others are mostly safer at a minimum of 50 °F (10 °C) or preferably higher. The less succulent species and those with non-succulent leaves will need a little water occasionally. All Euphorbias grow very well from seed but some species do not root easily from cuttings and the majority can take a month or so to root. They should be allowed to callus for 7–10 days or so, more if the cut section is a broad one.

Common Name Crown of Thorns.

Faucaria tuberculosa Schwant. $\times 1\frac{1}{2}$

faukaria tuberkulosa
Family: Ficoidaceae

Habitat Faucarias are to be found over a very wide area of Cape Province, South Africa, growing from sea-level up the mountain sides, but usually below an altitude at which frosts are likely to occur.

Description Faucarias are very succulent plants, usually clustering, forming into low growing clumps, with each head or rosette made up of 6 or 8 leaves. These highly succulent leaves only occasionally exceed 1 in. (2·5 cm) in length. They are somewhat triangular in shape, tapering to a point, whilst the upper surface is either flat or concave. The edge of the upper surface is usually armed with a number of soft teeth, varying in length from species to species. The leaves themselves can be smooth, turbercled, a plain green colour in many shades, or they may have creamy-white dots, sometimes arranged in transverse lines as in *F. tigrina*. The flowers which appear from the centre of each rosette in the autumn to early winter vary from $1\frac{1}{2}$ to $2\frac{1}{2}$ in. (3·8–6·25 cm) in diameter, usually in varying shades of yellow, although white does occur occasionally.

Cultivation Faucarias are ideal plants for the beginner and for the window-sill collector provided they are in a sunny position. Equal parts of sand and humus suit them very well. They require water from spring to autumn, but if over-watered they tend to grow rather unnaturally large. In the winter they are quite safe down to 40 °F (5 °C) or even lower for most species, provided they are dry.

Fenestraria rhopalophylla N.E. Br. ×2

fenestraria ropalofila
Family: Ficoidaceae

Habitat Fenestrarias are native to very dry regions in the north-western part of Cape Province, South Africa as well as to South West Africa.

Description They are very dwarf and exceedingly succulent plants, consisting of a cushion-like mass of cylindrical leaves about 1 in. (2·5 cm) long. These greenish leaves have a rounded or convex windowed tip some ¼ in. (6 mm) across which has given the genus its name *Fenestraria* and is the only part visible above the sand. This window varies its clarity according to weather conditions so as to obtain optimum conditions for photosynthesis and the plants can therefore endure intense light and heat. The flowers are usually borne on the perimeter of a plant on stalks up to 2 in. (5 cm) long. The flowers themselves vary from 2 to 3 in. (5–7 cm) in diameter. In *F. aurantiaca* they are in varying shades of yellow.

Cultivation Fenestrarias require a very sandy compost, at least 2 parts of gritty sand to 1 of humus, and should be planted so that almost the entire leaf surface is above soil level. About a 1 in. (2·5 cm) layer of coarse grit is essential around the plants to ensure good drainage round the neck. They can be grown under lightly shaded glass or in full sun. In the spring only very light watering or mist spraying is required; in summer and autumn a little more water is needed, whilst in the winter they should be kept dry. A minimum temperature of 45 °F (8 °C) is usually sufficient.

Ferocactus fordii B. & R. ×2

ferokaktus fordie
Family: Cactaceae

Habitat *Ferocacti* are native to the south-western U.S.A., that is Texas, New Mexico, Arizona, the southern part of California, and the Baja California part of Mexico, including some of the islands in the Gulf of California, and they also live in a wide area of central and northern Mexico. They are usually to be found in well drained locations on rocky and stony ground, but some species also grow in rolling grassland and amongst thorn bushes of various kinds. In some cases seedlings have germinated between some rocks, and once the plant has become a few feet in height it may fall over if the rocks are removed, as in such locations the root system is very poor.

Description The genus *Ferocactus* was erected by Britton & Rose to include many species which had been previously collectively grouped in the genus *Echinocactus*, and the name *Ferocactus* refers to the ferocious spination of these fine plants. They are globular to cylindrical, up to 9–10 ft (2·7–3 m) in height in some cases, and as much as 2–3 ft (0·63–1 m) in diameter, solitary or clustering. The rib structure is very prominent, but this is not always apparent in young plants. Sometimes they still have a tubercled appearance up to ten years of age; after this the tubercles merge to form the prominent rib structure. The rib count can vary from about 8 to 30 depending on the species, and as the plants grow and expand the rib count also increases to allow for the increased girth. The areoles are usually fairly large, and the spination is also very varied with radial and central spines: between 10 and 20 spreading radials which are often curved, and 1–4 centrals which stand out from the plant. All the spines are strong; radials can sometimes reach 3 in. (7·5 cm) in length while the centrals are often hooked quite strongly at the tip. They are longer than the radials and in *F. rectispinus* are nearly 6 in. (15 cm) long. The flowers appear as a ring on fairly new areoles near the centre, and in many cases a series of rings. The flowers are bell-shaped, 2–3 in. (5–7·5 cm) in diameter, and in many colours, including greenish yellow, orange, red and violet. The fruits are usually somewhat egg-shaped, up to 2 in. (5 cm) long while the dried remains of the flower stay attached on top. The exterior of the fruit is scaly, and when ripe it dehisces by means of a basal pore (opening at the bottom) so that the fairly large black seeds can run out.

Cultivation *Ferocacti* are easy plants to grow, normally raised from seed. This is not difficult, as some attractive spiny plants can easily be raised in 3–4 years, although in most cases they have to be a great deal older to reach flowering size. Most species grow well in a soil mixture of about equal parts sand and humus, watered from spring to autumn reasonably well. In fact during very hot weather it would be difficult to over-water, but always allow the soil to become almost dried out before re-watering. Young plants up to ten years of age are best grown under lightly shaded glass, but from then on extra light can be beneficial. In winter most species are safe down to 45 °F (8 °C) or even a little lower, provided they are dry. One species in particular, *F. latispinus*, can develop orange spots under high humidity conditions below 45 °F (8 °C), so be careful with this one.

Common Name Barrel Cactus.

Gasteria liliputana v. Poelln. ×3

gasteria lilipootahna
Family: Liliaceae

Habitat Gasterias are native to most of South Africa, particularly in Cape Province and South West Africa, usually growing in the shade of other bushes, from sea-level up to the cooler mountain slopes.

Description Gasterias are mostly small, stemless plants, usually freely clustering, with the leaves forming a rosette arranged in two opposite rows, in one plane (referred to as distichous). The leaf count per rosette can vary from 6 to 20. The leaves are usually a smooth, glossy dark green with paler cream markings. Occasionally they are reddish, or rough surfaced, e.g. *G. verrucosa*, and are from 1½ to 10 in. (3·8–25 cm) long. The leaves have an equal width along much of their length. They are pointed or rounded towards the tip, flat, slightly concave or convex on the upper surface, but distinctly convex on the lower surface. The leaf edges are usually smooth, but very tough. The flowers, which are tubular with a swollen base (shaped rather like an amphora), are from ½ to 1 in. (1·25–2·25 cm) long, in pastel shades of cream and pink, with both colours present, shading from one to the other. The flowers are produced on a simple unbranched flower spike, semi-erect, 6–18 in. (15–45 cm) long. The stem of the flower spike is pale green with a glaucous bloom.

Cultivation Gasterias are exceedingly easy plants to grow, though not exactly fast growing, and they are very suitable for use as house plants, particularly as they do not have to be grown on a sunny window-sill, but can be kept on one facing away from the sun. They will grow in almost any reasonable soil, with plenty of water from spring to autumn, and in winter in the greenhouse the temperature can fall to 40 °F (5 °C) or even lower with complete safety, provided they are dry. In the greenhouse they are best grown in a well shaded position, such as on the floor beneath the staging. If kept in the house where the average winter temperature is nearer 70 °F (21 °C) they will need water at intervals to prevent leaves dying back from the tips. This will happen normally with the oldest leaves, but it can happen to some of the others, if the plants are kept too dry in winter under such conditions. They are easily grown from seed or from leaves or even pieces of leaves.

Footnote The species illustrated is in fact the smallest species known, hence its specific name of *liliputana*. Gasterias have been in cultivation for a very long time, and there are many unnamed hybrid plants in cultivation which defy identification. There are also some very worthy hybrids between *Gasteria* and *Aloe*, called Gastroleas, and these require much the same cultivation treatment.

Glottiphyllum arrectum N.E. Br. ×2

glotifilum arektum
Family: Ficoidaceae

Habitat Species within this genus are to be found over a wide area of Cape Province in South Africa, particularly in the Karoo area, growing in stony and sandy situations.

Description Glottiphyllums are very low growing plants, and many species have somewhat larger and much more succulent leaves than the plant illustrated. These very succulent leaves form in pairs, with up to 3 or 4 pairs per head. Each leaf usually has a slightly obliquely flattened upper surface and rounded lower one. Some species have brilliant green leaves, while others are quite pale with a pinky-blue bloom on them. The flowers which appear singly are wide, opening up to 3 in. (7·5 cm) in diameter, more often than not in shades of yellow, but occasionally white. The main flowering period is the autumn and early winter, but occasionally flowers appear at other times, and last for 7–10 days.

Cultivation They are mostly very easy growing plants, and many species are very suited to sunny window-sill conditions, provided they are grown in a sandy humus mixture. Plants can become unnaturally large if watered too much, and this is one of those rare instances when under-watering gives best results. Light watering only is needed in the spring, but more should be given as the main flowering season approaches. Grow them under lightly shaded glass, whilst in winter if they are dry most species will stand near freezing conditions.

Greenovia aurea Webb & Berth. $\times \frac{1}{3}$

grenovia auria
Family: Crassulaceae

Habitat This genus is only found within the Canary Island archipelago, growing on mountain cliffs and barranco walls from 1,000 to 7,000 ft (300–2,133 m) in altitude.

Description Greenovias are stemless rosette-type plants, fairly freely clustering and when flowering takes place the rosette dies, to be replaced by the small rosettes which usually surround it. The rosettes vary from 1 to 10 in. (2·5–25 cm) in diameter when in growth, as the rosettes are rather open compared to the tight cup-like formation of the resting stage. The exception to this is *G. aizoon*, the green-leaved species where the rosettes remain almost fully expanded even in the hot resting period. The leaves are quite fleshy, very variable in size, rounded at the end but still with a slightly pointed tip. They are chalky blue usually tinged with pink, except in *G. aizoon* which has fresh green leaves. Flowers appear when the rosette elongates into a flower spike, which is from 6 to 18 in. (15–45 cm) in height, consisting of from 6 to 36 actual flowers. These are yellow, about $\frac{1}{4}$–$\frac{1}{2}$ in. (0·6–1·25 cm) in diameter.

Cultivation Unlike the Aeoniums to which they are closely related, and which share the same late-autumn to early-spring growing period, these plants prefer to rest during the hotter summer months in partial shade. They will grow in any reasonable soil and need average water through much of the year, including the summer resting period. In winter a temperature of 45 °F (8 °C) is best, with a little water.

Gymnocalycium hypobleurum var. ferox Bckbg. ×2

jimnokalisium hipobloorum (variety) ferox

Family: Cactaceae

Habitat Gymnocalyciums are native to a wide area of South America on the eastern side of the Andes range of mountains from the southern tip of Argentina to Paraguay, Uruguay, southern Brazil and Bolivia. They are to be found from sea-level to a few thousand feet up (1,000 m or more), sometimes growing amongst grass in a well drained soil and also amongst rocks. *G. gibbosum* var. *nigrum* is the one species which can stand freezing conditions as it is native to the southern Patagonian part of Argentina.

Description These plants are globular or very short-cylindric, usually solitary, a few sparingly clustering. They are fairly dwarf and many species are of a flattened globular habit, up to 6 in. (15 cm) in diameter. They are strongly ribbed, with up to 20 ribs (often far less), which are straight or slightly spiralled and are often noticeably tubercled (notched into warts) beneath the areole position. The woolly aereoles are $\frac{1}{4}$–1 in. (0·6–2·5 cm) apart, bearing up to 12 spines which are in many cases divisible between radials and centrals. These spines which can vary from grey to brown or black in colour are often curved, spreading in all directions, and tending to flatten against the plant. They are usually between $\frac{1}{2}$ and $1\frac{1}{2}$ in. (1·25–3·8 cm) long. As a general rule most of the curved spines spread to the sides or downwards, and there are rarely more than 3 centrals, when present. The flowers in most cases are funnel-shaped and open wide, the exception being species such as *G. mihanovichii* and *G. schickendantzii*. Otherwise when open wide the size can vary from 1 to 3 in. (2·5–7·5 cm), and the flowers vary in colour, with shades of green, white, yellow and red. The egg-shaped fruit like the exterior of the flower tube is scaly, smooth, without spines or bristles and is up to $1\frac{1}{2}$ in. (3·8 cm) long, green, red or purple when ripe.

Cultivation Gymnocalyciums are in most cases easy plants to grow, although rather slow from seed for the first two years, as many species develop quite big root systems during that period. *G. mihanovichii* is a very small growing species with many varieties, and can be flowered in $2\frac{1}{2}$ years from seed with ease, whereas most others take from 4 to 6, some even longer than that. They require as a general rule a soil of about equal parts humus and sand, reasonable amounts of water from spring to autumn during warm weather, and should be grown under lightly shaded glass even as old plants. Gymnocalyciums vary in body colour from species to species; many are in shades of green, whereas others can be reddish brown or a dark slate colour. The latter varieties can stand full sun treatment as older plants rather better. Most species can be kept in winter at a minimum of 40 °F (5 °C) if they are dry, with the exception of *G. mihanovichii* and its varieties, for which a minimum of 45 °F (8 °C) is low enough.

Footnote Gymnocalyciums seem to be very trouble-free plants, rarely troubled with pests, and guaranteed to flower freely each year in most cases. A variegated form of *G. mihanovichii* var. *friedrichiae* is on sale in the form of grafted plants, which are bright red or yellow. As the stock on which they are grafted is invariably of a quick-growing but tender type, a minimum of 50 °F (10 °C) is required in the winter. This variety is often named var. *rubra* which is incorrect: it should be 'forma Hibotan'.

Graptopetalum pachyphyllum Rose. ×3

graptopetalum pakifilum
Family: Crassulaceae

Habitat Members of this genus grow mainly in Mexico on mountain slopes and cliffs, while a few species extend into Arizona.

Description Graptopetalums, like Echeverias, are either stemless plants or dwarf shrubs up to 10 in. (25 cm) high, which often tend to sprawl and become rather pendant. The fleshy leaves are pointed or rounded at the tip and are $\frac{1}{2}$ to 3 in. (1·25–7 cm) long. They come in shades of blue, green and pink with a powdery bloom. Some species have one flower but most have 6–20 blooms well separated on a branched stalk. The flowers, which have a prominent tube, open wide and have 5 spotted or irregularly marked petals. The base colour is usually white, cream or yellow, with the darker markings in brown or purple.

Cultivation Graptopetalums are quite easy to grow and are suitable as house plants. Like the related Echeverias and Dudleyas they need a sand and humus soil mixture of about equal parts, and should be grown under lightly shaded glass. They need average watering during spring and early summer; later on if there is enough sunshine and less water is given they will develop their brilliant leaf colours. The miniature species, especially those with a very dense rosette, should not be over-watered and are best left dry in the winter. The shrubby species can have a little water if they are kept above 45 °F (8 °C); otherwise they can be left dry at 40 °F (5 °C) or below.

Harrisia fragrans Small. $\times \frac{1}{2}$

harisia fragrans
Family: Cactaceae

Habitat Harrisias are chiefly native to the southern half of Florida, the islands of the West Indies, and as far south as Argentina, growing either as dense thickets or scattered amongst other larger growing trees, even in near jungle conditions.

Description Harrisias are erect, columnar plants when young, but as the stems are mostly fairly slender, around 2 in. (5 cm) in diameter, they soon start to sprawl, supporting themselves on other bushes and trees. Most species have rounded ribs, and vary between 5 and 11 in number, with the areoles about 1 in. (2·5 cm) or less apart. The spines, which stand fairly erect, rarely exceed 1 in. (2·5 cm) in length, and often much less. The white funnel-shaped flowers, often with a fairly slender tube, can be as much as 8 in. (20 cm) in length, and are invariably highly scented, appearing during the summer. The fruits are usually quite large, 2–3 in. (5–7·5 cm) in diameter, yellow or red in colour.

Cultivation Harrisias are very easy to grow, enjoying a soil rich in humus, preferably two parts humus to one part sand, and they require plenty of water for all the warmer weather from spring to autumn. In winter a minimum temperature of 45 °F (8 °C) is advised, but for some of the West Indian species and those from Florida a minimum of 50 °F (10 °C) is preferred. These species may need occasional water during the winter to prevent undue shrivelling.

Haageocereus acranthus Werd. & Bckbg. × 1¼

hahgioserius akranthus

Family: Cactaceae

Habitat *Haageocerei* are native to the dry coastal cliff areas of Peru, bordering on the Pacific Ocean, and to the hills and valleys of central Peru above Lima.

Description *Haageocerei* are beautifully spined erect columnar cacti, in most cases, rarely exceeding 5 ft (1·5 m) in height. The stems vary from 2 to 3 in. (5–7·5 cm) in diameter. They cluster freely, usually from the base, giving a candelabrum effect. The ribs are distinct and are usually low, rounded, and between 14 and 20 in number. The areoles which are set quite close together on the ribs are woolly but variable in colour, bearing numerous spines from ½ to 1½ in. (1·25–3·8 cm) long consisting of radials and centrals (although in some cases it is difficult to distinguish between them). The spines are fairly fine, with a few exceptions, but are relatively stiff, and up to 40 in number, ranging from golden yellow to many shades of brown, sometimes black tipped. Many of the species are so densely spined that they completely mask the stem colour. The nocturnal flowers, in shades of white to pink, appear from areoles on the upper parts of the stems, with a 3–4 in. (7·5–10 cm) slender tube, but they open wide as illustrated. The outer surface of the tube has greenish-brown scales and a few hairs. In many cases, like the genus *Cephalocereus*, the areoles from which the flower buds appear become much more woolly or hairy and this is termed a 'pseudocephalium'. The fruit is globular to oval in shape, 1–1½ in. (2·5–3·8 cm) in length, and also has scales and hairs, but it is fleshy within.

Cultivation *Haageocerei* are all very handsome species, easy to grow from seed or cuttings, but not quick growing, although free root-run conditions do help in this respect to a certain degree. They enjoy a sand and humus compost of about equal parts, with average water from spring to autumn. Young plants should be grown for the first three or four years under lightly shaded glass, but once the spination becomes fairly dense they can safely be grown in full sun provided they are not too near the glass. Older plants can also be given rather more water during very hot weather, without any fear of rotting occurring. For the winter months they should be left dry, and a minimum of 45 °F (8 °C) is quite sufficient.

Footnote *Haageocerei*, rather like Espostoas and many of the *Ferocacti*, are grown for their attractive formation and superb spine colours, as they take many years even under ideal conditions with a free root-run to reach flowering size from seed. The only way a delay of perhaps twenty years from seed can be avoided is to graft a young plant on to a strong, quick growing *Cereus*. Three to four years' growth can then be achieved in one year!

Hoya australis R. Br. ×1½

hoiya ostralis

Family: Asclepiadaceae

Habitat This genus occurs mostly in the Far East, including India, Malaysia, Thailand and China, and a few grow in the East Indies and Australia, usually in semi-jungle conditions, supporting their stems on various trees.

Description The majority of Hoyas are climbing plants with fleshy leaves, but there are a few pendant species such as the well known *H. bella*, which is quite a miniature compared with most other species. In this case the leaves which are oval, tapering to a point are rarely more than ½ in. (1·25 cm) in length, but most other similar-shaped leaves measure 2–3 in. (5–7·5 cm) in length and 1½–2 in. (3·8–5 cm) across at the widest point. The twining stems and the leaves are of the same colour in varying shades of green, with the veining in the leaves showing up slightly darker. These fleshy leaves are quite tough, with a somewhat shiny surface. The newest part of the twining growths is usually leafless to start with and purplish in colour, later changing to green when the leaves appear. The flowers appear from a peduncle (a short stalk-like projection), from which the clusters of flowers appear not just once, but every year. It gradually grows longer, and should never be removed after the flowers have dropped off. The flowers, like those of other members of the family Asclepiadaceae, are 5 lobed, star-like in appearance, usually about ½ in. (1·25 cm) across, and are produced on reddish stalks from 1 to 2 in. (2·5–5 cm) in length. The centre of the flower (corona) is often reddish or pink, whereas in many species the lobes (petals) are in shades of white and cream, smooth or velvety surfaced. There are exceptions, including green or purple flowers, but they are not common in cultivation at present. The flower clusters usually last for 2–3 weeks and if seed pods appear they are like a pair of horns, but this rarely occurs in cultivation.

Cultivation Hoyas are exceedingly easy plants to grow, preferring a soil containing plenty of humus, preferably 2 parts of humus to 1 of sand. They need plenty of water from spring to autumn, when they should be grown under shaded glass. Direct sun in this period can burn the leaves. In winter, however, this does not matter, as there is usually insufficient strength in the sun to do any harm. A minimum temperature of 50 °F (10 °C) is advisable for most species, and they should be kept dry. If they are grown indoors or in a greenhouse suitable for growing the more delicate orchids, where the minimum temperature is nearer 70 °F (21 °C), some water will be required to prevent shrivelling of the leaves, or even complete leaf loss. *H. carnosa*, however, will stand cooler winter conditions if dry, even down to 40 °F (5 °C).

Footnote Many of these species can be grown as pot plants with small trellis arrangements attached to the pot or pushed into the soil, on which they can be trained. *H. carnosa* will grow and flower very well by such a method, and if it gets too large it can always be trimmed back to a manageable size.

Common Name Wax Plant.

Huernia transmutata Wh. & Sl. ×2

hernia transmutahta

Family: Asclepiadaceae

Habitat This genus is to be found over a wide area of South Africa and South West Africa, also in countries in west, central and east Africa, and up into southern Arabia. Most species, like most of the other dwarf Stapelieae, are usually to be found growing beneath other bushes for shade. They also grow beneath thorny shrubs for protection from animals which would otherwise eat them in time of severe drought. Finally a few species grow in rock crevices, e.g. *H. hallii*, which is often found among quartz outcrops. This is a very low growing species and comes from a particularly hot and arid area.

Description Huernias are low growing, freely clustering plants, with 4–5 angled stems with quite prominent, short but finely tipped teeth at intervals along these angles. These teeth are usually soft, but in many forms of *H. hystrix* they are hard and quite sharp. The stems vary from $\frac{1}{2}$ to 4 in. (1·25–10 cm) in length and $\frac{1}{4}$–$\frac{3}{4}$ in. (0·6–2 cm) in width and are smooth surfaced. They vary in colour from many shades of green to greenish purple and reddish purple, plain or slightly mottled, e.g. *H. macrocarpa*. The stem angles can be quite rounded or rather square, depending mainly on whether they are 4 or 5 angled species. There are two species with a greater number of stem angles, or with their tubercles in lines, rather like the rib structure of many cacti, and they are *H. distincta* with 8 or 9 tubercles and *H. pillansii* with 20–24. *Huernia* flowers are exceptionally variable. They have 5 lobes and there are also 5 teeth or sinus positions, which stick out between each corolla lobe. This is very prominent with some species and is clearly visible in the illustration. The flowers can vary from $\frac{1}{2}$ to $2\frac{1}{2}$ in. (1·25–6·3 cm) in diameter and are fleshy like all Stapelieae flowers. They may be campanulate, some with a lengthy tube for their size, or may open out very wide with only a small tube. The 'lifebuoy' Huernias and some other species have a raised annulus (lifebuoy-like ring) surrounding the mouth of the tube. The corolla tube and lobes may be smooth or covered with papillae (stiff hairs), whilst the colour may vary from cream to all shades of red or purple, plain, spotted or with irregular transverse lines. The separation of this very varied genus is again based on the central corona structure within the flower.

Cultivation Most Huernias are very easy to grow and will do exceptionally well in a humus and sand mixture of about equal parts, with plenty of water from spring to autumn during hot weather. They should be grown under lightly shaded glass. There are often exceptions to the rule when dealing with a genus in general terms, and the three most notable exceptions are *H. hallii*, *H. pillansii* and *H. verekeri*. These require a much sandier compost and far less water. In winter most species are quite safe down to 45 °F (8 °C) and can be kept fairly dry, but occasional water can be given in warmer spells to prevent undue shrivelling. However, the three above-mentioned species are best kept under rather drier conditions, or with high atmospheric humidity at a slightly higher minimum temperature.

Footnote Those who only have small greenhouses would be well advised to concentrate on a genus such as this, as they are not invasive plants but are very free-flowering from late spring to late autumn and the flowers, although not huge, are very varied.

Common Name Carrion Flower.

Hatiora salicornioides B. & R. $\times 1\frac{1}{2}$
hatiora salikornioides
Family: Cactaceae

Habitat A fairly dwarf epiphytic genus, native to the jungle areas of Brazil.

Description This is usually a very freely branching erect bush, but when the slender stems eventually reach 10 in. (25 cm) in length, they tend to arch over. These pale green cylindrical stems are divided up into sections (joints) which are sometimes rather bottle-shaped, particularly if the plant has been grown slowly. The areoles, which are few, bear short white bristles. The funnel-shaped flowers are less than $\frac{1}{2}$ in. (1·25 cm) in diameter, varying from yellow to orange. The fruit is very small, white when ripe.

Cultivation This is a very easy growing genus, which enjoys a soil containing a high percentage of humus, and should be treated as for *Chiapasia nelsonii*. However, like the hybrid Epiphyllums, these species do not require a high winter minimum temperature: 45 °F (8 °C) or a little lower is quite sufficient.

Footnote You may sometimes see the generic name as *Hariota*, but the correct spelling is *Hatiora*.

Hylocereus cubensis B. & R. $\times \frac{1}{5}$

hiloserius kubensis
Family: Cactaceae

Habitat *Hylocerei* are native to the West Indies, the semi-jungle areas of Mexico, Central America, Venezuela and Brazil. Although they inhabit wooded areas, they are not usually epiphytic but grow on the ground. The stems, however, support themselves on trees by means of aerial roots.

Description *Hylocerei* are truly climbing cacti, with 3-angled (winged) jointed stems. The margins of the angled stems are sometimes undulating (crenate), with the areole positions between the undulations. The spines are very few, exceedingly short and sometimes absent. The large funnel-shaped flowers are white or creamy white, nocturnal, highly scented and up to 12 in. (30 cm) long. Fruits are red and in *H. undatus* can be up to 5 in. (12·5 cm) across.

Cultivation All species are exceedingly easy growing, enjoying a soil rich in humus with plenty of water from spring to autumn. They should be grown under partially shaded glass. Most species require a minimum winter temperature of 50 °F (10 °C) or a little higher, otherwise they are prone to 'orange-rot' which can quickly disfigure a fine plant. However, the species illustrated will stand a temperature of 45 °F (8 °C) or even lower, provided it is kept dry.

Footnote Under suitable conditions with warmth and humidity they can flower at any time of the year.

Common Name Queen of the Night.

Kalanchoe farinacea Balf. f. ×2

kalankoi farinasia
Family: Crassulaceae

Habitat This genus has a widespread distribution over much of Africa, except the north, Arabia, Madagascar and most of the islands in the Indian Ocean, eastwards through India, Sri Lanka (Ceylon), Malaya and the East Indies. A few even grow in tropical America. Few species are to be found in areas where the temperature falls below 50 °F (10 °C) for any length of time but some are found in full sun locations or beneath other forms of vegetation and trees, sometimes even in quite moist tropical climates.

Description There are a few miniature species, such as *K. rhombopilosa*, which grows as a branched shrublet rarely exceeding 3 in. (7·5 cm) in height. Others are large erect plants up to 6 ft (1·8 m) high, e.g. *K. beharensis*, which is completely unbranched whereas others form quite dense clustering bushes or just sprawl around. Like Crassulas and Euphorbias they show tremendous variation so that any detailed description of the plant would be quite useless, as the leaves can be plain or irregularly marked, large and small, smooth or velvety. However, the flowers do have a basic structure which is easily recognisable. The flowers appear either singly, in small clusters, or as large upstanding inflorescences of a hundred or more tubular flowers. The individual flowers can be erect or pendant, $\frac{1}{2}$ in. (1·25 cm) to nearly 2 in. (5 cm) in length, but always appear as a slightly 4-angled corolla tube with short, but slightly recurved lobes. These flowers can be smooth or slightly velvety, in delicate or brilliant hues and are often somewhat fleshy in texture, so that in some species they last for a few weeks.

Cultivation Kalanchoes are again very easy plants to grow, and mostly enjoy a soil with at least a 50 per cent humus content and plenty of water from spring to autumn. Only a few of the miniature species should be given a more porous compost, and watered to a lesser degree. They can be grown under lightly shaded glass, or in full sun provided they are not too near so that they suffer leaf-burn. In winter the majority of species require a minimum temperature of 50 °F (10 °C) and a little water occasionally to prevent too much leaf fall. There are species which will stand cooler, drier conditions, but they are in the minority.

Footnote Although some species grow quite large, new smaller plants can easily be produced by cuttings or leaf-cuttings and some of the smaller growing species will flower very freely on a sunny window-sill. These plants produce an abundance of seed and some can flower within eighteen months.

Lapidaria margaretae Dtr & Schwant. ×2

lapidaria margareti

Family: Ficoidaceae

Habitat This monotypic genus is native to the Great Namaqualand region of South West Africa, where it grows in sandy and very stony soils or in rock crevices.

Description This plant is another dwarf stemless *Mesembryanthemum* which clusters in age, and grows in huge clumps like some related genera. Each head usually consists of 6–8 pairs of very succulent leaves, which are up to $\frac{3}{4}$ in. (2 cm) long and less than $\frac{1}{2}$ in. (1·25 cm) across at their widest point. The upper surface is flat, whilst the lower is very convex and is so shaped that the leaf is fatter towards the tip than at the base, with a rather triangular appearance. The angle lines on the leaves are somewhat cream coloured but the rest of the leaf surface is usually a pale greyish pink. The flowers appear singly, on a stalk about 1 in. (2·5 cm) long, opening wide up to 2 in. (5 cm) across. The petals are narrow, the centre of the flower filled with numerous stamens, and the colour is always a rich yellow.

Cultivation This genus is far from common in collections, and yet despite what has been written about it by some people it is quite easy to grow, even from seed. It can usually be flowered from seed in three or four years, and in a climate where there is a much longer growing season than in Britain it flowers in an even shorter space of time. *L. margaretae* requires a sandy humus soil mixture, grows and flowers well under lightly shaded glass, and needs less than average water at all times from spring to autumn. However, in the winter, provided it is kept dry, a temperature down to 40 °F (5 °C) is quite safe. In habitat this plant usually stands full sun conditions, although invariably the sandy soil in which it grows tends to drift over the plants and give them a little protection during the hottest period.

Footnote We grow the majority of our Mesembryanthemums, whether they are of the shrubby or stemless type, in shallow raised beds in the greenhouse. If this method is to be used, it does not mean that only species in the same genus can be grown together, but you must try to select kinds of similar growth-rate and water requirements. *L. margaretae* could be grown in a shallow bed of a rather sandy compost along with the following genera mentioned in this book: *Aloinopsis*; *Argyroderma*; *Cerochlamys*; *Conophytum*; *Lithops* and *Pleiospilos*. Our instructions vary a little for some of these genera, but with care they can still be grown together, even if the odd plant is given a little extra water by itself. The genus *Fenestraria* has to be treated far more carefully, whereas a shrubby plant like *Oscularia* would soon swamp other genera and for preference requires a richer soil.

Lithops lesliei N. E. Br. ×2

lithops lesliye
Family: Ficoidaceae

Habitat This genus is native to a wide area of South West Africa, also across the Orange River in the Namaqualand region of Cape Province, whilst the species illustrated is to be found in the Orange Free State and the Transvaal. They occur from sea-level to 5,000 ft (1,500 m) but the majority of species inhabit very dry regions, growing either in very sandy soil where they disappear beneath the sand as protection from the burning sun, or in rock chinks and amongst quartz outcrops. The species illustrated and *L. aucampiae* which also occurs within the Transvaal are sometimes found amongst grass in a soil which holds the moisture rather better than the almost pure sand in which the genus is found in South West Africa.

Description A single-headed *Lithops* plant consists of a pair of very succulent leaves, of which the top surfaces are roughly shaped like a semicircle, with the flat sides facing one another. The sides of the leaves are usually smooth, but quite variable in colour and sometimes of a different colour from the top surface, which can also be smooth, spotted or irregularly marked. The marks are often raised above the rest of the leaf surface. A few species have an almost windowed surface, irregularly patterned. The leaves can vary from shades of green to grey, pink and many shades of reddish brown. Each head produces a single flower from between the pair of leaves, which when opened to the average diameter of 1 in. (2·5 cm) almost obscures the head, which in only a few cases exceeds 1 in. (2·5 cm) across. The flowers, which are normally either yellow or white, appear in the late summer and early autumn and are often sweetly scented, opening in the mid-afternoon and closing before dusk.

Cultivation *Lithops* plants can easily be raised from seed, most species flowering in their third or fourth season. The majority of species require a soil mixture of about two parts gritty sand to one of humus, and although they are very small plants they should not be grown in too small a pot, otherwise their roots can become too hot and be lost. All our plants are grown under lightly shaded glass, even though in nature most species endure full sun conditions, but we have found them just as free-flowering by this method. In the spring when they are still really dormant, only very light overhead spraying is required, just enough to keep the roots alive but not sufficient to start the plants into growth, as the leaves must dry up completely before new ones appear from between them. More water can be given during the summer and autumn, and they should be left dry during the winter when a temperature even down to 40 °F (5 °C) is safe.

Footnote Most species of *Lithops* form into clumps, some into quite large clumps of 10 or 20 heads. *L. lesliei* is usually yellow flowered, but occasionally white occurs.

Common Name Stone Plant.

Islaya solitaria Rauh & Bckbg. ×1½

islaya solitaria

Family: Cactaceae

Habitat This genus is native to dry stony or rocky areas of southern Peru and northern Chile, up to about 3,000 ft (900 m).

Description Islayas are usually solitary, globular or short-cylindrical plants, up to 8 in. (20 cm) or so in height, although one species, *I. grandis*, can reach two or three times that height. Their diameter is usually about 4 in. (10 cm). The head is ribbed, with between 15 and 20 ribs, but the white woolly areoles on the ribs are raised, giving some species almost a tubercled appearance. The body of the plant is chalky blue or grey-green, whilst the spines, white to brown with darker tips, are rarely more than ½ in. (1·25 cm) long and often much less. The 1 in. (2·5 cm) diameter flowers are usually in shades of yellow, often with reddish-brown outer petals, particularly on their exteriors. Fruits when fully developed are 1–2 in. (2·5–5 cm) long, bright pink. They appear some weeks after the flowers have finished.

Cultivation Islayas in general require a very well drained compost, consisting of at least two parts of gritty sand to one of humus and a clay pot should be used so that the soil mixture will dry out quickly after watering. The soil mixture should be more porous if a plastic pot is used. These plants should never be over-watered and no water should be given in dull weather in the spring to autumn period, when they prefer top-shelf treatment in the greenhouse under lightly shaded glass. In winter keep them dry at 45 °F (8 °C).

Mamillopsis senilis Weber. × 1
mamilopsis senilis
Family: Cactaceae

Habitat This genus with only two species is native to the high mountain areas of Durango and Chihuahua in Mexico, where they sometimes endure snow in winter.

Description These plants have globular or slightly cylindrical heads, freely clustering, strongly tubercled, but masked by the spines (white in *M. senilis* and straw-coloured in *M. diguetii*). These consist of up to 40 spreading radials less than 1 in. (2·5 cm) long, fine and straight, and up to 6 more erect centrals with a hooked tip. Flowers are tubular, but open wide. They are up to $2\frac{1}{2}$ in. (6·3 cm) long, brilliant red in colour, appearing from the axils, which are between the tubercles. Fruit is small, slightly elongated, red when ripe, with a smooth exterior.

Cultivation Although these plants come from a high altitude up to 7,500 ft (2,500 m) or more, and endure snow, they are very prone to rotting through over-watering in a damp climate such as that of Britain unless considerable care is taken. They require a rather sandy humus mixture, with less than average water at all times, and should be grown under lightly shaded glass. In winter they must be kept dry, but in temperate climates where atmospheric humidity can be a problem a minimum temperature of 45 °F (8 °C) is safer. Those living in a climate where the winters are cold but dry will not have these problems and can allow the winter minimum temperature to be much lower.

117

Melocactus melocactoides DC ×2
melokaktus melokaktoides
Family: Cactaceae

Habitat *Melocacti* are native to almost all the tropical islands of the West Indies and the coastal regions of Central America, including southern Mexico, Venezuela and Brazil. In some cases plants grow exceedingly near the sea, and are quite tolerant even of the salt in sea spray. Some species such as *M. intortus* grow in a clay and leafmould mixture, whereas most of them grow in a very sandy soil, sometimes almost pure sand. There is the odd inland species such as *M. neryi* from Brazil.

Description *Melocacti* are globular to short-cylindrical plants, up to 3 ft (1 m) in height, but usually much less and having a diameter from 4 to 8 in. (10–20 cm). They normally remain solitary. They are distinctly ribbed plants with 9–20 ribs, usually straight, bearing oval areoles up to 1 in. (2·5 cm) apart, containing some wool. There are up to 15 spreading, slightly curved, radial spines, often less than this. The spines are up to 1 in. (2·5 cm) long, varying from white or grey to brown in colour. The centrals which are usually present in most species are 1–4 in number, usually standing out from the plant, and slightly longer than the radials which are of a similar colour. *Melocacti* are somewhat similar to *Cephalocerei* and *Haageocerei*, except that they produce a true cephalium which is terminal as depicted in this illustration. The cephalium is a compact mass of hair and bristly spines which develops on top, and from which the rings of small flowers appear. The colour of the bristly spines is often quite different from that of the strong spines lower down on the body of the plant. In many cases plants do not develop this terminal cephalium for perhaps ten or twenty years, so in early life the plant looks totally different, rather similar to other globular cacti. The flowers are very small, usually in brilliant colours, lasting but a few hours during the afternoon, but they are produced in abundance, often daily, over a period of many weeks or months during the summer and autumn. The fruits which appear later are rather elongated, smooth skinned, up to $\frac{1}{2}$ in. (1·25 cm) or more in height, often in shades of pink when ripe.

Cultivation *Melocacti* are not plants for the beginner, as they require in most cases a winter minimum temperature above the 50 °F (10 °C) mark, preferably nearer 60 °F (15 °C). They are shallow rooted plants, but produce long roots. Roots even as long as 9 ft (2·7 m) have been recorded, so they prefer a shallow pan-pot, rather than the more normal deep pot. All species should be grown in a sandy humus mixture, at least two parts of sand to one of humus, and watered with care at all times during the spring to autumn growing period. In dull cool weather during the growing period it is safer to refrain from watering at all, as they can rot very easily if over-watered and if the soil stays moist for too long. They are best grown on a top shelf under lightly shaded glass, whilst in winter they should be dry.

Footnote This genus has been included as a warning to many of our readers, as because of its unusual appearance many collectors new to the hobby want to grow it. Once you have the experience do try it, but it is easier to grow a plant without the cephalium to start with. If you buy a plant with the cephalium do ascertain that it has a perfect root system, otherwise it will almost certainly die.

Common Name Turk's Cap.

Monadenium schubei N. E. Br. ×1½

monadenium shoobie
Family: Euphorbiaceae

Habitat Members of this genus are chiefly to be found in East Africa from southern Tanzania northwards to Somalia, as well as in Rhodesia and Zaire (Congo). The most succulent species are to be found in the hottest dry regions, but others whose degree of succulence is far less grow in areas of higher rainfall where the temperature is still fairly high.

Description Monadeniums are another very variable group of plants, including the miniatures such as *M. rhizophorum* var. *stoloniferum*, which rarely exceeds 1 in. (2·5 cm) in height. It burrows a short distance and then another tiny stem appears bearing 2–4 small succulent leaves. There are other kinds which have very succulent tuberous root systems, producing either erect leaf-bearing stems or cylindrical snake-like stems, which are somewhat tuberculate with tiny thorns and fleshy leaves for part of their length. Then there are the shrubby or tree-like species up to 18 ft (5·5 m) in height such as *M. arborescens*. Like other genera within the family Euphorbiaceae these plants have milky sap. By far the majority of species have a swollen tuberous root system and in most cases the stems and leaves are a bright green colour. It is easy to identify these plants by their peculiar hooded flowers. Only a few species, such as *M. coccineum*, whose name signifies that it is red, can be described as attractive. The flowers, like those of most Euphorbias, consist of the basic elements necessary for reproduction. The flowers may be produced singly without any real stalk or may appear in a branched inflorescence. Some species, such as *M. echinulatum* and *M. magnificum* have unusual thorny green flower stalks which are quite long. In these hooded flowers the short stamens surround the base of the stalk on top of which is the ovary (which if pollinated produces a capsule with three compartments). It is topped off by the style which hangs down from the flower. See the accompanying illustration.

Cultivation For the majority of species a sandy humus soil mixture is required, with slightly less than average water at all times from spring to autumn, unless the weather is exceptionally hot, when extra can be given. A few of the thinner stemmed and taller growing species such as *M. laeve* can be grown in a soil containing more humus. The same applies to tall shrubby plants or those of more tree-like proportions. All of them, however, should be grown under lightly shaded glass for best results. In winter, however, a minimum temperature of 50 °F (10 °C) is essential for most species, and preferably a few degrees higher than that, particularly during any period when the atmospheric humidity is high. If they are kept too cold this extra humidity can be enough to rot plants completely. They should be left dry for the winter period. Some species if kept at a much higher minimum winter temperature may be given a little water, but be careful.

120

Mammillaria hemisphaerica Engelm. $\times \frac{1}{2}$

mamilaria hemisferika
Family: Cactaceae

Habitat This genus has a widespread distribution from sea-level to quite high altitudes from the south-west of the U.S.A. to Mexico, which is really its main home. It also grows in other Central American countries, down to Venezuela and a few of the islands in the West Indies.

Description Mammillarias are globular to short-cylindrical plants, solitary or very freely clustering, sometimes with many hundreds of heads. They have tubercles but these form into spiral rows, never straight rows. The sap of the plant can be clear or milky. There are usually numerous fine radial spines flattened against the plant and one or more longer centrals, slightly stronger than the radials, which are straight or hooked and stand out from the plant. Both kinds come in a great variety of colours. The flowers which appear in one or more rings just away from the centre of each head are $\frac{1}{4}$–1 in. (0·6–2·5 cm) in diameter, in almost any colour except blue, which never occurs in the family Cactaceae. Fruits are elongated, smooth, fleshy, in shades of yellow, orange or red when ripe and up to 1 in. (2·5 cm) long.

Cultivation It is almost impossible to give a general cultivation guide but the hooked spined plants which have larger flowers usually require a rather sandier humus soil mixture than the others, and also less water. Otherwise a soil of about equal parts sand and humus will suffice; grow under lightly shaded glass. During the winter a minimum temperature of 45 °F (10 °C) is warm enough, provided they are kept dry.

Common Name Pin Cushion.

Monanthes polyphylla Haw. ×1½

monanthes polifila
Family: Crassulaceae

Habitat Unlike the genus *Greenovia*, this one is native to all the islands within the Canary Islands. *M. brachycaulon* also grows on the Salvage Islands between Madeira and the Canaries. The plants are to be found growing from sea-level to nearly 7,000 ft (2,300 m), in rock crevices or as mounds on rocks.

Description They are all very dwarf plants, clustering to some degree, and species such as *M. polyphylla* and *M. subcrassicaulis* grow into immense clumps. The rosettes rarely exceed ½ in. (1·25 cm) in diameter when in full growth, whilst in the resting season they can be nearly half that size. The leaves are small, smooth or finely velvety but very succulent, and there can be a considerable number in each rosette. The flowers which vary from cream to greenish brown have from 6 to 8 very narrow petals. They are about ¼ in. (0·6 cm) in diameter and are borne on a branching stalk which may also be slightly velvety in texture.

Cultivation They are mostly easy growing species, enjoying a sand and humus mixture, with a slightly greater emphasis on the sand. They mostly prefer to be grown under lightly shaded glass, and they do not want intense heat during the summer, growing well on the floor of the greenhouse under the front of a staging. They require average watering, and although they are winter growers they adapt themselves to growing during our spring to autumn period. In the winter a temperature down to 40 °F (5 °C) is sufficient with a little water occasionally. However, under conditions of high atmospheric humidity in the winter a slightly higher temperature may be required to prevent damping off.

Monvillea saxicola Bgr. ×1

monvilia saxikola

Family: Cactaceae

Habitat Monvilleas come from quite a wide area of Argentina, Brazil, Paraguay and Peru. They grow in rather differing locations amongst other trees on which the weaker-stemmed species support themselves. One species which is native to a small island off the coast of Brazil – St Michael's Mount – grows and clambers over rocks.

Description Monvilleas are columnar slender-stemmed plants, night-blooming and in most cases highly scented. They are freely branching either from the base or further up their stems, and some species form into dense thickets of their own. The stems have from 5 to 9 ribs, rounded or more angled, bearing small circular areoles. Some species have plain deep green stems; others have attractive blue and white mottling, e.g. *M. marmorata* and *M. spegazzinii.* There are up to 10 fine radial spines, rarely more than $\frac{1}{2}$ in. (1·25 cm) long, often much less and varying in colour from white or grey to yellowish brown or black. The 1–3 centrals are longer than the radials, sometimes as much as 1 in. (2·5 cm). They are straight or slightly curved, standing out from the plant, and of a similar colour. The slender-tubed flowers, opening wide as illustrated, are produced very freely over the summer and autumn months, and are up to 5 in. (12·5 cm) long and 4 in. (10 cm) wide, white or pale pink in colour. Fruits are globular or distinctly elongated, from 1 to 3 in. (2·5–7·5 cm) long, reddish when ripe, fleshy within and smooth on the exterior.

Cultivation Monvilleas are exceedingly easy to grow, erect as young plants, but needing some support later. They enjoy a soil containing two parts of humus to one of sand, and plenty of water during the warmer months, from spring to autumn. Most species are best grown under lightly shaded glass. In winter a minimum of 50 °F (10 °C) is suitable for most species, provided they are kept dry. If kept at a higher temperature a little water may be required to prevent shrivelling.

Footnote Monvilleas are amongst the finest of the night-flowering *Cerei*, as although the blooms are not as gigantic as some of the *Hylocerei* and *Selenicerei*, they mostly flower very freely over a long period. Normally they flower through the summer and autumn, but our specimens which are grown under free root-run conditions flowered from April to October after the mild winter of 1973/74. There were few nights without one or more blooms open, and spreading their fragrance throughout one of our large greenhouses. This species has also been referred to as a variety of *M. cavendishii.*

Myrtillocactus geometrizans Cons. $\times 1\frac{1}{2}$

mertilokaktus jeometrizans

Family: Cactaceae

Habitat This genus is native mainly to Mexico, where it is to be found either on the tableland areas or in mountainous situations particularly in the region between San Luis Potosi and Oaxaca. One species, *M. cochal* is native to the Baja California region of Mexico, whilst *M. eichlamii* hails from outside Mexico in Guatemala.

Description *Myrtillocacti* are large growing cacti, freely branching and of a similar habit to many of the erect growing *Cerei*, but rarely attaining a greater height than 15 ft (4·5 m) and up to 4 in. (10 cm) or so in diameter. They are distinctly ribbed plants, but not so acutely ribbed as some of the *Cerei*. All of them have a very distinctive bluish-green stem colour, while in some species it is glaucous blue. There are usually 5–6 ribs, and the areoles are normally set from $\frac{1}{4}$ to 1 in. (0·6–2·5 cm) apart, depending on the species. In the case of the species illustrated they are well apart, whereas in *M. schenckei* they are close together, much larger and have black felt-like wool. The radial spines which vary from 5–8 are stout, less than $\frac{1}{2}$ in. (1·25 cm) in length, spreading, brown or black. The one central spine is even stouter than the radials, standing out from the stem, 1 in. (2·5 cm) or less in length and of the same colour. The flowers often appear in clusters from the upper areoles of stems, but in large plants they are quite small, rarely more than 1 in. (2·5 cm) long, funnel-shaped and opening wide. These nocturnal flowers are highly scented, white, or sometimes tinged with pink. The fruits are small, almost globular, blue when ripe.

Cultivation *Myrtillocacti* are as easy to grow as any of the *Cerei* and *Trichocerei* and will do well in any reasonable soil, with plenty of water from spring to autumn. However, in winter their requirements are quite different as they are prone to develop blemishes if the temperature falls too low, particularly when the air is damp. Ideally a minimum winter temperature of 50 °F (10 °C) should ensure that no unsightly marks appear, and plants can be left dry. With their attractive blue colour they can make pleasing house plants, but if kept indoors where the temperature never falls below 60 °F (16 °C) they will require occasional water to prevent shrivelling. Also in order to keep the attractive blue body colour they need as much light as possible, so a sunny window is called for.

Footnote Young plants of *M. geometrizans* raised from seed will appear to be almost spineless for the first few years, and it is because they grow quickly and are easy to handle that they are often used as grafting stock. The only snag is that no matter what has been grafted on to them, they will require a temperature in winter of 50 °F (10 °C) or higher.

126

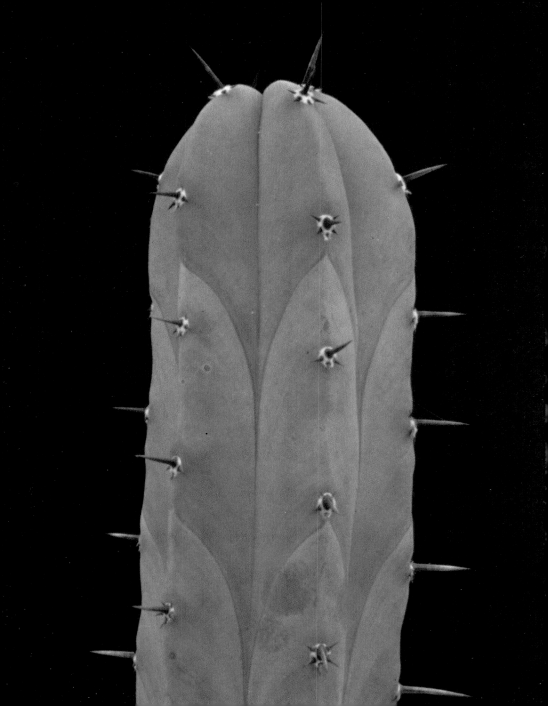

Neoporteria nigrihorrida Bckbg. ×1½

neoportaria nigrihorida
Family: Cactaceae

Habitat Neoporterias are native mainly to Chile. They always grow in well drained locations up to around 6,000 ft (1,800 m) and in some cases even higher, where a few species endure very dry but fairly cold conditions in the winter.

Description These are globular to short-cylindrical plants normally up to 4 in. (10 cm) in diameter, although in a few instances they can reach as high as 4 ft (1·3 m), e.g. *N. clavata*. Such a plant would be a great age as none of the species can be termed quick growing. They are distinctly ribbed with 10–20 ribs, which are straight but occasionally spiral slightly as in the illustration. The ribs are slightly tubercled in appearance as the areoles are usually raised on the ribs. The oval areoles which have a little wool are set around ¼–½ in. (0·6–1·25 cm) long. The radials are often curved, spreading somewhat against the body of the plant, whilst the centrals are also often curved like the radials, but stand out a little more from the plant. Their colour can vary from cream or golden to reddish brown and black, and in most cases all the spines are fairly strong, with the exception of species such as *N. gerocephala*, where they are fine and flexible. The flowers appear from the newer areoles near the centre, sometimes more than one developing from the same areole. They are funnel-shaped or they have an inner whirl of petals which do not fold back to any great degree and remain circling the stamens and pistil. These flowers are 1 in. (2·5 cm) or less in diameter, whereas the more open funnel-shaped kinds are up to 2 in. (5 cm) in diameter. The flower colour varies from cream to shades of red and violet; the smaller-flowered kinds stay open day and night for many days, whereas the larger ones close at night.

Cultivation Neoporterias are not difficult plants to grow from seed or keep as mature plants, provided they are grown in a sandy humus compost, and only watered liberally in very hot weather. At other times it is advisable to be careful, particularly with any species which have deep tap-roots. (This advice is worth remembering in connection with almost any other tap-rooted cactus.) They grow well on a top shelf under lightly shaded glass, and once they are of flowering size, which may take five years or more, the densely spined species can take full sun treatment. We have found, however, that even these kinds grow and flower very well under lightly shaded glass. In the winter they must be dry at all times, and will be safe even down to 40 °F (5 °C) or lower, but with high humidity it may be safer to keep them a little warmer.

Footnote There is considerable controversy among experts as to whether this genus should include other genera such as *Neochilenia*, *Pyrrhocactus*, *Horridocactus*, etc. which causes great confusion for the amateur. We should also mention that in addition to flowering normally in the spring some species may be expected to flower again in autumn.

Notocactus megapotamicus Ost. ex Hert. ×2

notokaktus megapotamikus

Family: Cactaceae

Habitat *Notocacti* are native to southern Brazil, northern Argentina, Uruguay and Paraguay, growing either in stony or sandy ground, but also on grassy hillsides where the soil is of a sandy nature.

Description *Notocacti* are quite variable in form. Some are small, flattened globular plants; others become somewhat columnar in age. The largest of these is the well known *N. leninghausii* which can reach 3 ft (1 m) in height and a diameter of 4 in. (10 cm). The smaller-growing species have a lesser diameter. *Notocacti* are solitary or freely clustering and possess a ribbed structure, but these ribs which number anything from 10 to 30 are very low in most cases, notched into low warts on which the small areoles are positioned. The areoles are set quite close together, bearing up to 20 bristle-like radial spines usually between $\frac{1}{4}$ and $\frac{1}{2}$ in. (0·6–1·25 cm) long, varying from white or yellow to shades of brown. There are up to a maximum of 6 central spines, also fairly thin, often slightly curved and standing out from the plant. They are up to twice the length of the radials and of a similar colour. Some species such as *N. haselbergii* and *N. scopa* have such dense spination that the body of the plant is almost completely obscured. The flowers which appear from near the centre of the plant can vary from as small as $\frac{1}{2}$ in. (1·25 cm) across (in *N. haselbergii*) to as large as 3 in. (7·5 cm). These are usually funnel-shaped, but some open very wide and are from red to yellow in colour. The outside of the flower towards the base is scaly with hairs and bristle-like spines of a similar colour to those on the main part of the plant. The bristly fruit is fairly small, dry within when ripe.

Cultivation *Notocacti* are very easy to grow, and the majority of species can be grown to flowering size within three years; many of them are particularly attractive even without flowers, because of their spination. They grow well in a soil of about equal parts sand and humus, needing plenty of water from spring to autumn during warm weather, and should be grown beneath lightly shaded glass. In winter if kept completely dry they are safe down to 45 °F (8 °C) or even lower for some species.

Footnote The genus *Notocactus* is one of those most suited to the person just starting to grow cacti, as many species can be grown and flowered on a sunny window-sill. Plants named as *Brasilicactus* also belong under *Notocactus*.

Opuntia basilaris var. ramosa Parish. × 1½

opoontia basilaris (variety) ramosa
Family: Cactaceae

Habitat Opuntias have perhaps the widest distribution of any genus within the family Cactaceae. They are to be found from sea-level to 12,000 ft (2,750 m) from Canada, throughout the U.S.A., West Indies, Galapagos Islands, much of Central and South America, down to the southern tip at Tierra del Fuego in Patagonia. Some specimens endure temperatures below 0 °F (−18 °C), while some species from the West Indies cannot stand temperatures near freezing.

Description This genus can be divided into three groups: *Platyopuntia*, which has pads similar to those in the illustration; *Cylindropuntia*, which has cylindrical stems instead of flat ones; and *Tephrocactus*, a low growing plant with numerous short oval stems or joints. Opuntias include miniature kinds which grow in low clumps, prostrate varieties and others with large tree-like dimensions. The areole positions on all Opuntias, no matter which type, bear glochids, which are small barbed bristles, usually in clusters. Some Opuntias, like that illustrated, have glochids only, whereas others have one or many spines, often very long, and these are also barbed. The colour of the glochids and spines varies from white to reddish brown or black and they may be of different colours. They are fairly easily detached and sometimes the joints become detached when the spines are caught in an animal's fur or on a human's finger. This is one way in which nature ensures the propagation of a species. The flowers are borne from the areoles. In Platyopuntias they usually sprout from the edges of the pads in profusion. They are of all colours except blue and some species have flowers of varying colours. The flowers usually open wide, lasting for two days. The base of the flower is the ovary, which if the flower has been fertilised will swell and contain numerous hard and relatively large seeds amidst the flesh. When the flower has finished it withers away and drops off, leaving a circular depression on the upper end of the otherwise egg-shaped fruit. When ripe these fruits take on various colours from yellow to red and purple. The outer surface is covered with glochids, so it must be handled with care.

Cultivation Opuntias are with few exceptions very easy plants to grow, and most of them require a soil that contains a reasonable percentage of humus, but many could be grown in ordinary garden loam. Most species grow best under lightly shaded glass when young, but can take full sun after three or four years and need plenty of water during warm weather from spring to autumn. It is impossible to lay down a minimum temperature as a general guide as this depends on the origin of the species and its normal climatic requirements. However, with the exception of a few tropical species, most species are quite safe down to 45 °F (8 °C), but many kinds will not be harmed by freezing temperatures, provided they are dry.

Footnote Opuntias are often commonly referred to as 'Prickly Pear', 'Fig Cactus' or 'Indian Fig'. The fruits of many species are eaten, particularly those of one of the larger growing species, *O. ficus-indica*.

132

Oreocereus doelzianus Bckbg. ×1

Orioserius dolzianus

Family: Cactaceae

Habitat Species within this genus are to be found on the slopes of the Andes mountains in Argentina, Bolivia, Chile and southern Peru up to an altitude of 9,000 ft (2,750 m), often growing in very rocky and stony ground.

Description *Oreocerei* have fairly erect columnar stems rarely more than 3 ft (1 m) high, often branching freely from the base in age. The stems consist of 9–17 rounded ribs, with a horizontal groove between each pair of areole positions. The areoles bear stiff spines as well as hair, and in some species this forms so densely that the green body of the plant is completely obscured. The flowers appear from areoles near the top of a stem, or from those at the crown as in the species illustrated. These are tubular, in varying shades of red and magenta, up to 3 or 4 in. (7·5–10 cm) long and remain open for two days. Fruits are small, globular, usually slightly hairy, and dehiscing by a basal pore.

Cultivation *Oreocerei* are popular plants in cultivation, being grown for their appearance rather than for the flowers, as specimens have to be many years old to reach maturity. They require a reasonably well-drained soil mixture, plenty of water during hot weather from spring to autumn, whilst in the winter they should be kept dry at a minimum temperature of 45 °F (8 °C). If the atmospheric humidity is very low, they will be quite safe at lower temperatures as they are basically mountain cacti. The densely hairy species in nature endure freezing conditions at night at certain periods; however, the degree of humidity is very low. In cultivation young specimens grow best under lightly shaded conditions, whereas older mature specimens endure full sun, even when grown in tropical regions. Once specimens are four or five years old, best results are obtained under free root-run conditions where their roots can spread in all directions rather than within the confines of a pot. As a general rule *Oreocerei* are not particularly prone to insect pests once they are past this age.

Footnote *O. doelzianus* Bckbg, is also known under the name *Morawetzia doelziana* Bckbg.

Common Name Old Man of the Andes.

shaded glass. They need plenty of water from spring to autumn. In winter the minimum temperature should not fall below 50 °F (10 °C) and occasional water is needed.

Pediocactus knowltonii L. Bens. ×2

pediokaktus noltonie

Family: Cactaceae

Habitat *Pediocacti* come from as far north as Idaho and Montana, down to New Mexico and Arizona, growing often at fairly high altitudes from between 4,000 and 10,000 ft (1,200 and 3,000 m).

Description *Pediocacti* range from globular to short-cylindrical, solitary to freely clustering, but are always quite dwarf in habit. Each head is tubercled and there is no rib structure. The spines are often flattened against the plant and are ¼–1 in. (0·6–2·5 cm) long, needle-like, but very variable in colour. The flowers appear from near the centre of the plant, varying from ½ to 1 in. (1·25–2·5 cm) in diameter, and are shaped like funnels in white or pale shades of cream or pink. The fruit is small, egg-shaped and smooth, and yellow-brown when ripe.

Cultivation Although some *Pediocacti* come from very cold locations where they endure snow and severe freezing in winter, it is imperative that all species are grown in a well drained compost, particularly if plastic pots are used in preference to clay. A soil mixture of two parts gritty sand to one of humus is safest, and should always be watered with care. We find *Pediocacti* grow and flower well when grown on a fairly high shelf in the greenhouse, but under lightly shaded glass. In winter all the species will be quite safe at 40 °F (5 °C) or even lower if dry. *P. simpsonii* and the variations of it can be grown in the open air, in a raised bed as used in alpine gardening, with a very porous soil mixture, even where winter temperatures drop below 0 °F (−20 °C).

Pereskia aculeata Mill. × 1½
pereskia akuliahta
Family: Cactaceae

Habitat Pereskias are chiefly native to the West Indies, Central America and South America.

Description Pereskias are virtually leafy shrubs or trees with a very woody main stem, while bearing spines in pairs in the axils of the leaves. The leaves are deciduous, sometimes slightly succulent, of varying shapes and up to 3 in. (7·5 cm) in length. The highly scented flowers appear solitary or in panicles, opening very wide. They contain numerous stamens and come in yellow, orange or pink; they are 1–3 in. (2·5–7 cm) in diameter. The fruit is usually globular and smooth, 1–2 in. (2·5–5 cm) in diameter, and yellow when ripe.

Cultivation Pereskias are very easy to grow, require plenty of water from spring to autumn, and will succeed in almost any reasonable soil. Their root systems are quite extensive so that in due course a large tub will be required to house them, although a free root-run is preferable. Species which flower in late autumn will want enough warmth and water to develop before winter arrives. Watering can then cease and the leaves will drop. Many species can be wintered at 45 °F (8 °C) or lower once a woody stem has developed. Young specimens should be kept at 50 °F (10 °C) and given some water through the winter.

Footnote It is thought that cacti in general have evolved from Pereskias, as this is the least succulent member of the family Cactaceae.

Common Name Rose Cactus.

141

Peperomia asperula Rauh. $\times 1\frac{1}{2}$

peperomia asperoola
Family: Piperaceae

Habitat Peperomias are native mainly to South America, many species being non-succulent and native to the tropical forests as epiphytes. Those of interest to the succulent enthusiast come from somewhat drier locations in Argentina, Bolivia, Colombia, Paraguay and Peru.

Description Peperomias are low growing plants, rarely exceeding 6 in. (15 cm) in height and often much less, erect when young but tending to sprawl with age, freely branching. The branching can occur in two ways, either from near the base or from the point at which a stem had died back after producing its short terminal flower spike. The stems are very slim in species like *P. nivalis* but in species such as *P. dolabriformis* and the one illustrated they can be nearly $\frac{1}{3}$ in. (0·8 cm) thick. They are greyish green and sometimes brown with age. As is clearly visible in the illustration, these stems bear pairs of fleshy succulent leaves alternating, almost always with a concave windowed surface on top. *P. dolabriformis* has slim hatchet-shaped leaves in a vertical plane, whereas most of the other species correspond more to *P. asperula*. The leaves vary from green to a powdery greyish blue, but the windowed surfaces are always rather shiny. The flower spike is terminal from a stem tip, but is very insignificant, and can best be described at a cursory glance as being similar to a very slim pine cone, although in actual fact made up of numerous minute creamy-white flowers very close together.

Cultivation Peperomias are not difficult plants to grow, although a minimum temperature of 50 °F (10 °C) seems best if you want to grow a nicely shaped plant. A little water can be given to prevent leaf-drop or die-back on any of the stems. Peperomias grow well in a sand and humus soil mixture of roughly equal parts, under lightly shaded glass, with average water from spring to autumn. They are normally propagated from cuttings, which root quite easily within a week or so. Such cuttings need only be dried for 4–7 days before planting, depending on the diameter of the cut stem. As some species can become straggly, it is sometimes a good idea to cut off any flowering shoots so as to make a plant into a nice bush-shape.

Footnote There are quite a number of Peperomias in cultivation, often seen as house plants, but these are usually only semi-succulent, and have somewhat different leaf structure to those mentioned above. Such species require rather more water than the species listed here. One interesting point is that with many Peperomias, if the leaves are crushed between one's fingers the smell is similar to that of aniseed.

Pleiospilos bolusii N. E. Br. ×1½

pleospelus boloosie
Family: Ficoidaceae

Habitat The majority of species within this genus are to be found within the confines of Cape Province, South Africa. A number of them inhabit the Karoo region but one species, *P. borealis*, hails from the Orange Free State. Most species grow in very sandy or stony soil in low rainfall areas, generally at lower altiudes.

Description *Pleiospili* are another very succulent-leaved member of the stemless *Mesembryanthemum* group, most species slowly forming into groups of a few heads. Each head consists of one to two pairs of leaves, and on occasion, three or four. The leaves are very thick in some species, as seen in the one illustrated, and can be up to 3 in. (7·5 cm) in length and width. The upper surface is flat, but the lower surface is very convex and the leaf-tip can be blunt or acute. The leaves of some species are distinctly elongated, and although the leaf surface can be either smooth or slightly rough, in all instances the entire surface is covered with translucent dots. The flowers appear in the autumn or early winter. They emerge singly or up to 4 in succession from between the same pair of leaves, measuring as much as 4 in. (10 cm) across. The centre of the flower is always filled with a mass of yellow stamens. The petals themselves are always narrow, as in the illustration, and vary in colour from pure white to shades of yellow or orange-yellow, growing paler towards their bases. The flowers are often highly scented, not unlike the smell of coconut.

Cultivation Most species are quite easy to grow, but in common with some of the genera in this group, they can easily be over-watered and then become bloated, far exceeding the size that they attain in nature. They can be grown in a soil of about two parts gritty sand to one of humus, with less than average water at all times from spring to autumn, in order to produce a more typical plant. In the winter when a temperature even down to 40 °F (5 °C) is quite satisfactory they should be left dry. We have most of our specimens growing under free root-run conditions, and by this method have found that some species will continue flowering from August nearly to Christmas as the Glottiphyllums do. These plants can stand full-sun growing conditions, but very good results are obtained under lightly shaded glass.

Footnote Most members of the *Pleiospili* develop very strong root systems in the form of strong, lateral tap-roots, and consequently the pot size should not be too small. However, when plants are being repotted it is advisable to trim some of the roots back, so that the next pot need not be so large. If you do trim them back, leave the plants on a bench for about a week in a warm but slightly shaded position, so that the cut root ends can callus.

Piaranthus foetidus var. diversus N. E. Br. ×1½

piaranthus foitedus (variety) diversus
Family: Asclepiadaceae

Habitat Members of this genus are to be found over a wide area of Cape Province in South Africa and also in South West Africa. They inhabit rather similar locations to the Duvalias mentioned earlier, growing usually beneath bushes in sandy soils.

Description These are very similar to Duvalias as regards their vegetative appearance, as they are prostrate growing plants made up of numerous small egg-shaped joints 1–2 in. (2·5–5 cm) long and ½ in. (1·25 cm) across at the widest point. These joints or stems are usually 4 or 5 angled, green or green-brown in colour, smooth, but slightly tubercled with 4 or 5 small teeth along each angle. The flowers appear in late summer and autumn, in clusters, on stalks ½–1 in. (1·25–2·5 cm) long. As with other Asclepiads the flowers are usually 5 lobed, star-like, and around 1 in. (2·5 cm) across. The upper surface of the lobes is usually slightly pubescent (velvety texture), and cream, yellow, dark purple or a mixture of these in colour. The seed pods are a pair of horns, containing wind-borne seed.

Cultivation All the species are easy to grow and flower, doing well in a sand and humus mixture of roughly equal parts. They grow best under lightly shaded glass with average watering from spring to autumn. All the species can be safely wintered at a minimum of 40 °F (5 °C) if kept dry.

Common Name Carrion Flower.

Pyrrhocactus bulbocalyx Bckbg. ×1

pirokaktus bulbokalix

Family: Cactaceae

Habitat *Pyrrhocacti* are native chiefly to northern Argentina and also to the other side of the Andes in Chile, growing as high as 9,000 ft (2,750 m) in well drained locations.

Description *Pyrrhocacti* are solitary, globular or short-cylindrical plants, with an average of 12 to 20 distinctly marked rib edges. The round or oval areoles are quite large, and since they are raised on the ribs, have a notched appearance. The spines are very strong, somewhat thicker towards their bases, and are generally in clusters of between 10 and 20, clearly divisible into radials and centrals. The radials are slightly shorter than the centrals and spread out against the plant, whilst 1–4 centrals stand out from the plant and are between 1 and $1\frac{1}{2}$ in. (2·5–3·8 cm) long. The flowers are funnel-shaped, many constricted half-way up as illustrated, and appear from near the centre in shades of yellow and red, 1–$2\frac{1}{2}$ in. (2·5–6·3 cm) long.

Cultivation *Pyrrhocacti* are fairly slow growing plants, and as such require a compost with a fairly high proportion of sand, with average watering during hot weather from spring to autumn. However, during cool dull weather at that time of year watering should cease. Also if plastic pots are used a more porous soil mixture is advised. *Pyrrhocacti* grow well on a top shelf under lightly shaded glass during the growing season. In winter if kept dry they are quite safe down to 40 °F (5 °C).

Rathbunia alamosensis B. & R. ×1

rathbunia alamosensis
Family: Cactaceae

Habitat Rathbunias are native to the hot dry regions of Mexico, mostly in Sonora and Sinaloa, forming dense thickets.

Description Young Rathbunias will grow erect up to perhaps 6 ft (1–8 m) like many Harrisias, but will then bend over and branch freely in all directions. The cylindrical stems have from 4 to 8 rounded ribs, and can vary in diameter from 1 to 3 in. (2·5–7·5 cm). There are 10–16 spines on average, stiff, with radials spreading, while 1–4 centrals stand erect. The spines vary in colour from grey to brown. Flowers are rather unusual, appearing near the tops of stems in the form of a slightly scaly tube with bristle-like spines in the axils. The flowers are tubular up to 4 in. (10 cm) in length. The petals tend to roll back against the tube, so that the style and the numerous stamens can emerge. Tube and petals are of varying shades of pink and red. The fruit is globular, 1–1½ in. (2·5–3·8 cm) in diameter, red, and slightly spiny.

Cultivation Although coming from somewhat drier locations than many species of *Harrisia*, in cultivation the *Rathbunias* enjoy much the same treatment as regards soil, water and winter temperature. If they are kept at 45 °F (8 °C) and lower in the winter, and the degree of humidity is high, orange spots can develop which will quickly spoil a fine specimen. Rathbunias will flower in summer when they are 18 in. (45 cm) high.

Rebutia spegazziniana var. atroviridis Bckbg. ×2

rebutia spegaziniahne (variety) atroviridis
Family: Cactaceae

Habitat Species within this genus are to be found chiefly in the north-western part of Argentina and in Bolivia, growing amongst grass and in rock crevices up to 10,000 ft (3,050 m) or so.

Description Rebutias are small-growing plants, usually clustering, with either flattened globular or short-columnar heads. They are not distinctly ribbed plants, but the areole positions are very slightly raised and often arranged in a spiral formation as with Mammillarias. The flowers are small, funnel-shaped, last for two days (diurnal), and are normally produced from around the base of each head. Few flowers exceed 1 in. (2·5 cm) in length or diameter, but they are produced in a tremendous range of colours and shades with the exception of blue, which is the one colour never to be seen in any true cactus. They appear in spring and early summer.

Cultivation Rebutias are very easy growing plants, ideal for the window-sill and enjoy a soil rich in leafmould, with plenty of water in warm weather from spring to autumn. In winter if kept dry they will stand quite low temperatures at or even below freezing. Young plants are best grown under lightly shaded glass.

Footnote The genus *Rebutia* now includes many other species which have appeared under other generic headings, including *Aylostera, Cylindrorebutia, Digitorebutia, Mediolobivia* and *Sulcorebutia*, as the differences are too slight for generic separation.

Rhipsalidopsis rosea B. & R. (Hybrid) $\times \frac{1}{2}$

ripsalidopsis rosia
Family: Cactaceae

Habitat The type species is native to the tropical forest areas of southern Brazil, where it grows in the forks of trees and is a truly epiphytic cactus.

Description *R. rosea* and the various hybrid forms are somewhat shrub-like, very freely branching, erect in the first few years but becoming pendant in old plants. The flattened joints, bearing a few bristle-like hairs at the areole positions, are rarely much more than 1 in. (2·5 cm) long, and vary in colour from a greenish blue with tinges of purple, depending on how much sun a plant has received. The 1½ in. (3·8 cm) long flowers appear from the ends of the joints in great profusion during late spring and early summer. The fruit is very small, smooth and purple in colour.

Cultivation *R. rosea* and the hybrid forms are exceedingly easy to grow, using a soil rich in humus, and can be treated in the same manner as *Aporocactus flagelliformis*. However, as they flower so abundantly and this takes a lot out of a plant, additional feeding with a liquid fertiliser as used for house plants is advised for some months after flowering.

Common Name Easter Cactus. This name is also used for another beautifully flowered cactus, *Schlumbergera*.

Sceletium compactum L. Bol. ×2

skeletium compactum
Family: Ficoidaceae

Habitat This genus is found over a wide area of Cape Province, South Africa, including the Karoo region.

Description Sceletiums are prostrate-growing shrubby Mesembryanthemums, growing into really large masses at times, and often re-rooting where the stems touch the soil. The thin stems are brown and woody, usually becoming grey with age, and bear branches of some 6–12 flat, slightly fleshy leaves. The leaves are always pointed at the tip, somewhat triangular in shape, around 1 in. (2·5 cm) long and up to $\frac{1}{2}$ in. (1·25 cm) wide at the widest point. As the stems increase in length and branch the leaves die but papery skeletal remains stay attached to the stem, as can be clearly seen in the accompanying illustration. The flowers, which are white, or shades of straw-yellow, and pink, appear either singly or sometimes as many as three together, and are often on stalks, varying from $1\frac{1}{2}$ to 2 in. (3·8–5 cm) in diameter.

Cultivation Sceletiums are exceedingly easy plants to grow, more often than not propagated from cuttings. They enjoy a soil of about equal parts sand and humus, and can be given a reasonable amount of water from spring to autumn, and grown under lightly shaded glass. In winter a minimum temperature of 40 °F (5 °C) is sufficient, provided they are kept dry.

Footnote Flowers appear during the summer and early autumn so any trimming should be carried out immediately after this, if a plant is becoming invasive.

Sansevieria trifasciata var. laurentii N. E. Br. ×⅓

sanseveria trifasiahta (variety) laurentie
Family: Agavaceae (formerly Liliaceae)

Habitat This genus is native particularly to tropical Africa extending from west Africa through to east Africa, down to Rhodesia and just into South and South West Africa. It also occurs in Arabia, Madagascar, India, Sri Lanka (Ceylon), and Burma. Species such as the thicker more cylindrical-leaved varieties grow in somewhat drier locations amongst rocks in sandy soil in areas of low rainfall. However, the plant illustrated originates from Zaire (Belgian Congo) where it grows in moister conditions although capable at certain times of standing drought. Many of the species grow in partially shaded positions, beneath other bushes. *S. thyrsiflora* has escaped from cultivation in Florida, and huge clumps can be found growing in quite dense shade.

Description Sansevierias are very fleshy-leaved plants, which usually develop new shoots by means of underground rhizomes, but some species, particularly the smaller growing ones, throw out runners. These produce a new shoot at their tips and later throw down roots anything from 1 to 3 ft (30 cm–1 m) from the parent plant. Each rosette can contain from 5 to 25 leaves, depending on the species, and be anything from 2 in. (5 cm) to 6 ft (1·8 m) in length. These leaves may be erect and flattened, as illustrated, with a width of just over 2 in. (5 cm), but quite thin. Some species such as *S. hahnii* have leaves of a similar thickness, but form into a rosette rather like an *Agave*, up to 6 in. (1.5 cm) across. The most succulent-leaved species are those with cylindrical tapering leaves, which at their widest point can be from ½ to 1 in. (1·25–2·5 cm) or more across. The leaves of all species are very tough, with smooth or roughened surfaces, sometimes very glossy. They are plain dark green or as illustrated, banded with irregular white or cream spots and markings and also a yellow variegated edge. The flowers of Sansevierias are not particularly interesting, usually opening at night. They are small and tubular in shape, cream or white coloured and sometimes beautifully scented. They are produced either on an erect flower spike or as a dense inflorescence at soil level, when a limited number of the flowers open each night and close by morning.

Cultivation Sansevierias are very easy plants to grow, provided the temperature in winter does not go below 50 °F (10 °C) as an absolute minimum, when the plants should be kept dry. They like a soil of about equal part humus and sand, and average water from spring through to autumn in warm weather. They should be grown under shaded glass, as the leaves can burn quite easily, particularly with the thinner glossy-leaved species. The more rough-surfaced kinds can take brighter light conditions without this fear. If these plants are being kept in centrally heated conditions where the temperature never drops below 70 °F (21 °C), a little water can be given to them during the winter very occasionally. If over-watered at this time of year they can quickly rot off at soil level, and in fact thrive on neglect during the winter months. They are easily propagated either by division of the rhizomes or division of sections of leaves; however, those variegated forms with yellow leaf edges can only be perpetuated by rhizome division. If propagated by leaf sections they revert to the normal plant without the yellow leaf margins. Divided rhizomes and leaf sections should be left for a week, before replanting into our suggested soil mixture.

Footnote Sansevierias, although commonly grown as house plants, for which they are particularly well suited are not well known in any great variety of species available to the public.

Common Name Mother-in-Law's Tongue.

Senecio crassissimus Humb. ×2

senesio krasisimus
Family: Compositae

Habitat Senecios are a world-wide genus of plants, containing well over a thousand species from annuals to perennial bushes and small trees. However, not all of them can be considered as truly succulent, although there are many border-line cases, as one would expect in a genus of this size. The majority of the succulent species are native to various parts of Africa and the islands around Africa, including the Canary Islands and Madagascar. (*S. anteuphorbium* occurs in Morocco.) Other Senecios are usually found growing at lower altitudes in sandy and rocky situations, sometimes (e.g. *S. kleinia* from the Canary Islands), very near the sea.

Description Some Senecios have quite swollen root systems, which are in themselves a means of storing water in times of drought, but basically the succulence in the Senecios which is of interest to us lies in the leaf or stem structure. Some species are creeping forms with quite fat spherical or egg-shaped leaves at intervals along the stems. These leaves have a windowed strip on the upper surface, and are usually a bluish-green colour. The species also throw down roots at regular intervals along their stems. The more erect growing and freely branching species can vary from 6 in. (15 cm) to as much as 6 ft (1·8 m) in height, and one species, *S. johnstonii*, grows even taller than that as an erect single-stemmed tree. It is one of the very few found at a high altitude, some 12,000 ft (3,650 m) up on Mt Kilimanjaro in Tanzania. *Senecio* leaves take on many forms: horizontally flattened or vertical as illustrated, smooth- and wavy-margined, cylindrical, tapering to a point, and so on, and are usually from 1 to 3 in. (2·5–7·5 cm) in length. The leaf colour is equally variable, including shades of green and plain or streaked bluish colours. Many have a powdery bloom on their surfaces and some have a hairy or velvety white surface. The stem succulent species usually have tiny leaves and cylindrical or angled stems. A *Senecio* flower consists of numerous small florets surrounded at times by petals of a similar colour as in the illustration. These are often absent, e.g. in *S. stapeliaeformis*. The colour can vary from white or cream to orange and red.

Cultivation Senecios are mostly easy growing plants. The larger variety will grow in any reasonable soil, but some of the smaller species and also the succulent stemmed kinds prefer a somewhat better drained mixture, so a sandy humus mixture is advisable. They require water from spring to autumn, large amounts in very hot weather, although the stem succulents need less, while in winter they should be left dry. Most species are quite safe down to 45 °F (8 °C) in winter, with the exception of some of the east African and Madagascan species where a minimum of 50 °F (10 °C) is preferred. Many of the smaller growing species make fine house plants. If they get too big, it is an easy matter in most cases to make a smaller new plant from a cutting, provided it has been dried for about seven days before planting.

Sinocrassula yunnanensis Bgr. ×2

sinokrasula yunnanensis

Family: Crassulaceae

Habitat This genus is entirely native to the mountainous regions of China and India, such as the Himalayas. It grows at high altitudes in rock chinks where light frost and some snow occurs during the winter period, but is always in well drained positions.

Description These plants are very dwarf, clustering in habit, and of a loose mat formation. Some species such as *S. densirosulata*, are very tender to touch and will easily drop to pieces, with each leaf rooting and growing into a new plant. They are either biennial (flowering and dying in two years or seasons), or perennial. The rosettes which rarely exceed 1 in. (2·5 cm) in diameter, can consist of from 20 to 50 or more small leaves, quite fleshy, oval and pointed. The leaf colour can vary from grey-green, to bluish pink to olive-brown, sometimes covered with irregular darker markings. The leaf surface can be smooth or pubescent (velvety). The flower spike, which is formed by an elongating rosette, can vary from less then 3 in. (7·5 cm) to as much as 8 in. (20 cm) in height. It is multi-branched, and bears numerous tiny semi-globular flowers which range in colour from grey to brown.

Cultivation These plants coming as they do from somewhat similar habitat conditions as the Sempervivums could be grown in a similar way, except that they are prone to rot off in wet winters. They should in fact be treated as cold-house subjects. The temperature may fall well below freezing, but since the plants are kept dry they can safely withstand it. However, unlike Sempervivums which tend to open up under heated greenhouse conditions in winter, Sinocrassulas do not. They can be grown quite happily on the floor of a heated greenhouse, so if you wish to try this, find the coolest spot, making sure that they receive direct sunlight. They will grow in any reasonable soil, but to keep the tight typical appearance of the rosettes, a well drained soil and careful watering are advised.

Footnote This genus is somewhat neglected today, but with the steadily spiralling costs of heating a greenhouse or conservatory, genera such as *Sinocrassula, Sempervivum* and *Sedum*, as well as the frost-hardy members of such genera as *Agave, Lewisia, Opuntia, Echinocereus, Neobesseya*, etc., will probably come into their own. One greenhouse 150 ft (45 m) long in 'The Exotic Collection' is devoted to this study. Species from many of the above genera are also grown in the open in raised rockeries.

Stapelia nobilis N. E. Br. ×⅔

stapelia nobilis

Family: Asclepiadaceae

Habitat This genus, which contains over a hundred species, is native to a very wide area of South and South West Africa as well as tropical Africa, and like the related genera included in this book is usually found beneath trees and bushes.

Description Stapelias are far more varied in size than any of the related genera mentioned so far, varying from very dwarf species with stems less than ¼ in. (0·6 cm) wide to some which exceed 2 in. (5 cm). Some of the larger species can produce stems up to 12 in. (30 cm) in height. They branch in many ways, either as close growing clusters, or burrowing in snake-like fashion, or, like *S. engleriana* and *S. revoluta*, branching mainly underground and producing new stems 6–12 in. (15–30 cm) apart. The stems are usually 4 angled, but 5 or 6 angled stems do occasionally occur. They may be glabrous (smooth) or pubescent (velvety) in surface texture, and in colour can be many shades of green, sometimes purple-tinged in places, and also a lovely chalky-blue colour. The flowers vary in shape, too, some opening out flat like a 5-lobed star, some bell-shaped, and, occasionally, some having corolla lobes rolled back behind the disc of the flower, as with *S. engleriana* and *S. erectiflora*. The size can vary from as small as ½ in. (1·25 cm) to as much as 18–20 in. (45–50 cm) in diameter, e.g. *S. gigantea*. The species illustrated can produce flowers, when well grown, from 10 to 14 in. (25–35 cm) across. Some species, have a raised annulus (lifebuoy-like ring) like that of Huernias. This even occurs in one of the commonest species, *S. variegata*. The flower surface can be smooth or rather rough, sometimes with raised transverse but irregular lines, and covered with stiff papillae (hairs), e.g. *S. pulvinata* with long coloured silky hairs. The seed pods, shaped like a pair of horns, are amongst the largest produced in the Stapelieae tribe, being up to 6 or 8 in. (15–20 cm) in length, and containing in some cases many hundreds of wind-borne seeds.

Cultivation The majority of Stapelias grow well under lightly shaded glass in a normal soil mixture of equal parts humus and sand. Provided the weather is hot, they will enjoy a reasonably plentiful supply of water from spring to autumn. There are a few species where a sandier compost is called for and less water. This applies mainly to the burrowing kinds, or those that branch below ground rather than above. In winter most species are quite safe down to 45 °F (8 °C) or even lower, but those from tropical Africa prefer a temperature above 50 °F (10 °C). If wintered at 45 °F (8 °C) or lower they can be kept dry, but otherwise a little water very occasionally will be needed to prevent undue shrivelling.

Footnote The main flowering period is during the summer and autumn, although many species will continue flowering as long as reasonable weather lasts.

Common Name Carrion Flower.

Strombocactus disciformis B. & R. ×2

strombokaktus diskiformis

Family: Cactaceae

Habitat This plant, the only one in this genus, is native to very stony ground in the State of Hidalgo in central Mexico, where it grows, like many of the species of *Ariocarpus*, with just the top surface exposed above the ground. Because of its body colour, often seeming even greyer in its natural surroundings, *Strombocactus* is very difficult to find when not in flower.

Description *S. disciformis* is a small growing, flat-topped, globular plant, solitary or sparingly clustering. It is made up of notched but rather flat tubercles, usually arranged in a spiral, giving the plant a ribbed appearance. Single heads rarely exceed 4 in. (10 cm) in diameter, whilst these flattened, angular tubercles bear a small white areole at the top. Some specimens are completely spineless, but when spines are present, they are fine and bristle-like, grey, and up to 4 in number. They tend to drop off after a few years, so that none are to be found towards the outer edge of the plant. The flower buds have grey to reddish scales, with narrow petals. The flowers open wide and are from 1 to 2 in. (2·5–5 cm) in diameter. In most cases the centre of the flower is pale yellow with the remainder being pure white, and it opens during the daytime. The fruit is very small, and of a brownish hue. When it ripens the tiny seeds spill out on to the surface of the plant.

Cultivation *S. disciformis* is one of those plants which, rather like members of the *Ariocarpus* and *Obregonia* genera, grow very slowly and are consequently bought by amateurs as plants of flowering size. It is almost a lifetime's work to raise one from seed to flowering size, and for the first few years they remain exceedingly small and need very careful attention. When they reach flowering size they do best under lightly shaded glass on a top shelf, although they are capable of growing in full sun. They require a rather sandy humus compost and should always be watered with care, particularly during cool weather in the spring to autumn period. In the winter, provided they are kept dry, they are quite safe at a minimum temperature of 45 °F (8 °C) or even a little lower.

Footnote Although *S. disciformis* is a rare and very slow growing plant, it should present no great difficulty to the ordinary amateur enthusiast, provided he purchases a plant which is already well rooted. It must not be over-watered and flowers usually in two bursts in midsummer and early autumn. We have had some specimens flowering on and off over a period of three or four months.

Thelocactus bicolor B. & R. ×1½

thelokaktus bikolor

Family: Cactaceae

Habitat *Thelocacti* are native to central and northern Mexico, and also northwards across the Rio Grande in southern Texas. They grow in locations varying from rocky stony ground to grassy areas in sandy-clay soil. They are sometimes found in the open, but more often than not beneath other larger cacti or some of the many kinds of low growing xerophytic trees which inhabit these areas.

Description *Thelocacti* are of globular or short-cylindric habit and fairly dwarf growing. However, one or two varieties such as *T. nidulans*, while only 6 in. (15 cm) or so in height, can be 10 in. (25 cm) across. Some species are solitary, but others are sparingly clustering in habit. They are distinctly ribbed plants, sometimes spiralled, and range in number of ribs from about 8 in the species illustrated, to as many as 20 in *T. nidulans*. The ribs are usually rather low, and although occasionally not easily defined, they are normally notched into raised angular or six-sided warts, or tubercles. The areole positions are somewhat elongated into a groove above the point at which the spines appear. There can be as many as 20 radial spines, generally needle-like, and spreading in all directions against the body of the plant. The spines are from ½ to 2 in. (1·25–5 cm) long, while the centrals tend to be thicker, up to 6 in number, and stand out from the plant from 1 to 3 in. (2·5–7·5 cm). A few species have woody-type spines which tend to split into fibres as they get older. *T. nidulans* is an example of this. Spine colour of both radials and centrals varies from white or grey to golden yellow or dark reddish brown. The flowers which appear from the new areoles in the centre of the plant are funnel-shaped, opening wide from 1 to 3 in. (2·5–7·5 cm) in diameter, and varying in colour from white to shades of yellow, pink and purple. The fruit is small, globular, and dry. It dehisces by a basal pore so that the seeds run out of the bottom on to the plant and the ground.

Cultivation *Thelocacti* in general are easy growing plants, although many species may take five or more years to reach flowering size. They require a mixture of about equal parts sand and humus, a reasonable amount of water from spring to autumn if the weather is warm, and lightly shaded glass. The denser spined species and those with a chalky-grey body can be grown in full sun once they are beyond the seedling stage, provided they are not too near the glass. This does not apply to the green-bodied ones. In winter most species are safe at a minimum temperature of 45 °F (8 °C) or even a little lower, provided they are kept dry.

Footnote Seeds of *Thelocacti* are relatively large for cacti seeds, and they are easy to germinate. As seedlings for their first 2–3 years be careful not to over-water them as their root systems are not extensive and should not be moist for too long.

Common Name Texas Pride.

Toumeya lophophoroides Bravo & Mshll. ×2

toomaya lofoforoides

Family: Cactaceae

Habitat Toumeyas are generally found in well drained rocky or stony ground situations, with only the top of the plant visible. A number of species are to be found in the San Luis Potosi area in northern Mexico, the kinds which are grouped by some authorities under another generic name, *Turbinicarpus*. A few other Toumeyas such as *T. papyracantha*, *T. peeblesiana* and *T. fickeisenii* are found in the U.S.A. in northern Arizona, New Mexico and southern Colorado. With the exception of *T. papyracantha*, which grows amongst grass, these species are also found in well drained rocky or stony ground situations.

Description Toumeyas are all miniature growing plants, solitary or sparingly clustering, usually globular and up to 3 in. (7·5 cm) in height. However, *T. papyracantha* is cylindrical. Toumeyas average from 1 to 2 in. (2·5–5 cm) in diameter. The bodies are distinctly tubercled with such woolly areoles that the centres of the heads of some species seem a mass of wool. There are from 1 to 8 spines, from ¼ to 1 in. (0·6–2·5 cm) long, appearing flattened or papery. These often twist in various directions and are off-white to greyish brown in colour. In many cases there is no distinction between radials and centrals, except with *T. papyracantha* where there are usually about 7 distinct very short radials and 1 long papery central spine. The flowers which appear from the centre of the plant are funnel-shaped, ½–1 in. (1·25–2·5 cm) across, but sometimes the spines prevent the flowers from opening fully. This happens with *T. schmiedickeana*. The flowers vary from white to cream or pink, and usually have a darker median stripe down each petal. The fruit is small, globular and dry when ripe, and like the *Thelocacti*, the seeds are dispersed by means of a basal pore.

Cultivation Toumeyas are reasonably easy to grow, provided they are watered with care and have a sandy humus soil mixture. If the weather is really hot during the spring to autumn period they can stand more water. Like *Ariocarpus*, Toumeyas should be grown in clay pots as they must not remain moist for too long. They should be grown on a top shelf, under lightly shaded glass for best results in growth and spine formation. The flowering period within this genus is very long, from February onwards for *T. schmiedickeana*, to September and October for such species as the one illustrated. In the winter these plants should be kept completely dry, when a minimum temperature of 45 °F (8 °C) or even lower is quite safe. Even though *T. schmiedickeana* starts to flower in February, you should not start watering them unless you happen to live in a semi-tropical climate where watering requirements are of course different.

Footnote These plants are ideal ones for those of you with very small greenhouses, as they remain small and yet can be expected to flower very freely each year. *T, papyracantha* is often grafted on to other plants as it is more subject to rotting than the others.

Trichocereus huascha B. & R. $\times \frac{1}{3}$

trikoserius hwasha
Family: Cactaceae

Habitat Species within this genus are to be found in most of the countries within South America, in varying habitats and conditions, from sea-level to over 9,000 ft (2,750 m). Species from high altitudes endure frosts and snow, but survive these conditions by the generally low degree of humidity.

Description *Trichocerei* are quite varied in form. The very thick-stemmed columnar species branch in the form of an erect candelabrum. Alternatively, other species such as the one illustrated grow quite erect when young, but once branches start to appear from the base the older ones tend to sprawl. The columnar stems, varying from green to greenish blue, have a vertical formation of ribs which are usually rounded and 5–35 in number. The areoles from which the spines appear are sometimes woolly. The spine count per areole can be quite varied but the erect columnar species usually have very thick stout spines, whilst the others have much finer ones. The flowers, which usually appear from the upper part of a stem, are mostly very large, funnel-shaped, usually white, highly scented and nocturnal. The globular fruits can be an inch or so (a few centimetres) in diameter, rather spiny and hairy.

Cultivation *Trichocerei* are mostly very easy growing plants, and quite tolerant, as they will grow well in any reasonable soil. The thick-stemmed 'candelabrum' type, particularly those species from higher altitudes, tend to be the slower growing ones but can be grown in cultivation under the same conditions and receive the same treatment. These kinds will take full sun conditions without burning, whereas a few of the other species which are not so densely spined do best under lightly shaded glass. The growing season for these plants is from spring to autumn, when they enjoy plenty of water, particularly during hot weather. In the winter all species will be quite safe with a minimum temperature of 45 °F (8 °C) if dry, and many species are quite happy at much lower temperatures.

Footnote There is also a red-flowered form of *T. huascha* which is often listed as a *Lobivia*.

Sedum roseum Scop. $\times \frac{1}{3}$

sedum rosium
Family: Crassulaceae

Habitat This genus has a wider distribution than any other included in this book, except perhaps *Euphorbia*. The species come from some very cold parts of the world such as Alaska and Siberia, from most temperate regions, and from many parts of South, Central and North America. However, the real centres are central Europe, the Mediterranean region and Asia. Sedums grow from sea-level up to alpine regions.

Description Sedums may be annuals, but most species are perennials. Some kinds are prostrate growing, with swollen roots, including the species illustrated, which is hardy in frost and snow. There are many dwarf shrubs, while a few reach bush-like proportions of up to 6 ft (1·8 m) in height. The flowers usually appear in crowded rosettes measuring about $\frac{1}{4}$ in. (0·6 cm) across and made up of 6–7 petals varying in colour from white and yellow to shades of pink, red, violet and occasionally blue.

Cultivation By far the majority of Sedums commonly in cultivation can be treated as frost-hardy, but if you are uncertain try to find out the country of origin of the plant as this is a fairly reliable method of telling whether it is for the garden or the greenhouse. The few tender species generally cultivated in Britain, such as *S. humifusum*, will stand cold-house treatment, but cannot withstand wet and cold. The taller hardy species, often with larger leaves, will grow in an ordinary loam, whilst the smaller-leaved, compact species want a well drained rockery for best results.

Weingartia fidaiana Bckbg. ×2
wingahtia fidiyahna
Family: Cactaceae

Habitat Weingartias are mostly native to the arid slopes of the Andes mountain range in South America, particularly in Bolivia, northern Argentina, and just into Chile.

Description Weingartias are mostly globular, solitary to start with but produce a number of offsets when they reach maturity. They are ribbed plants, and in some cases deeply ribbed although this is not true of the species illustrated, which is one of the smallest members in the genus. Most species develop a succulent tap-root (of a tuberous nature) with a very narrow neck position between that and the head. The proximity of the circular or oval areoles from one another varies considerably, but all species have relatively stiff spines made up of 8–18 spreading radials, and up to 8 centrals which stand more erect. Their length can vary from $\frac{1}{2}$ to $1\frac{1}{2}$ in. (1·25–3·75 cm), with the centrals always slightly longer than the radials. The flowers appear from the top, but away from the actual growing point, in a ring. They have a short tube, beneath the funnel-shaped petal formation, and are less than $1\frac{1}{2}$ in. (3·75 cm) in diameter. In colour they are usually in shades of yellow or pale orange.

Cultivation These slow growing plants are easily grown from seed under lightly shaded glass in a deep pot with a soil of equal parts sand and humus. They need average water from spring to autumn and if kept dry are safe at 40 °F (5 °C) in winter. If humidity is high they should be kept slightly warmer.

171

Wigginsia (Malacocarpus) corynodes Salm.-Dyck. ×1½

wigginsia (malakokarpus) korinodes

Family: Cactaceae

Habitat This genus is native mainly to lower altitudes and coastal regions of Uruguay, Paraguay and southern Brazil, growing either in rocky well drained positions or on sloping ground amongst grass.

Description These plants are globular to short-cylindrical in form and quite dwarf in habit, not exceeding 8 in. (20 cm) in height and from 4 to 6 in. (10–15 cm) in diameter. They are distinctly ribbed, having each up to 20 ribs. These are straight or slightly spiralled, rounded or acute, but always notched in such a way that the areoles are in the depressions between the notches, ½ in. (1·25 cm) or less apart. There are up to 12 radial spines, ½–1 in. (1·25–2·5 cm) long, slightly curved, white or grey-brown towards the tip, and normally just 1 central spine 1 in. (2·5 cm) or less long of a similar colour. The areoles are exceedingly woolly when new so that the centre of a plant, as you can see in the species illustrated, gives a very white woolly appearance. The flowers are yellow, up to 2 in. (5 cm) across, appear together usually from the centre of the plant, and have a prominent red stigma in the centre of the stamens. The outside of the flower tube is covered with wool, scales and bristly spines. The fruits appear some weeks or even a month or so after the flowers have finished, pink in colour and up to 1 in. (2·5 cm) in length.

Cultivation Species within this genus are relatively easy to grow, and in most cases can be expected to flower within 4–5 years from seed. They require a sand and humus soil mixture of roughly equal parts and average water from spring to autumn. Watering should be stopped during the growing season only if there is a spell of particularly dull and cool weather. Wigginsias should be grown under partially shaded glass at all times. For the winter a minimum temperature of 45 °F (8 °C) is sufficient and a degree or so lower is unlikely to do any harm, provided it is dry.

Footnote We have listed these plants under the unfamiliar name of *Wigginsia*, though most people still refer to them under the older name of *Malacocarpus*. The change to *Wigginsia* took place in 1964 because the generic name *Malacocarpus* had been used since 1843 for a member of the family Zygophyllaceae. Wigginsias, like Opuntias possess sensitive filaments (the basal part of a stamen). When they are touched by an insect they close towards the style, dusting the insect with pollen which it will inadvertently take to another flower.

Wilcoxia poselgeri B. & R. ×2

wilkoksia poselgere
Family: Cactaceae

Habitat Wilcoxias are native to southern Texas as well as a varied range of habitats in Mexico, spreading from Coahuila to southern Puebla and Baja California. They invariably grow among other vegetation, especially thorn bushes, which support their slender stems. They are usually to be found at fairly low altitudes.

Description The stems are clearly ribbed and can reach 3 ft (1 m) in height and no more than ⅓ in. (0·9 cm) in diameter. The narrow ribs are rounded, up to 10 in number, and the areoles are sometimes set so close together that they form an almost interconnecting mat over the surface of the stem. In *W. poselgeri* the central spine is clearly visible. Other species have up to 14 radial spines ⅙ in. (0·5 cm) long and varying from white or grey to black in colour. One species which has very short stems is *W. schmollii*. This species has long white wool growing from the areoles. The flowers vary from 1 to 2 in. (2·5–5 cm) in diameter, are formed like wide funnels or have petals which roll back completely. They range in colour from white or pink to red, remaining open for two days. The fruit is oval and is up to 1 in. (2·5 cm) long, reddish green when ripe, slightly fleshy and covered with short spines.

Cultivation Wilcoxias have a dahlia-like root system, and as such require a large pot in cultivation to accommodate them. They need a slightly sandy humus soil mixture, enjoying plenty of water during warm weather from spring to autumn, and are best grown even as old plants under lightly shaded glass. In the winter they should be kept dry, a minimum temperature of 45 °F (8 °C) being sufficient for all the species.

Footnote Wilcoxias are wonderful flowering plants, their flowers often increasing in size the longer they remain open. They can be grown from seed or from cuttings, the latter developing within a year or so the typical dahlia-like root system. New plants can also be raised from divided tubers. This often happens in nature when during periods of drought the aerial stems die, or when animals such as goats eat them.

Common Name Dahlia Cactus.